Winning Investment Decisions

Winning Investment Decisions

Walter F. Wild, Ph.D.

To order additional copies of this book, contact:
Xlibris Corporation
1-888-795-4274
www.Xlibris.com
Orders@Xlibris.com
75962

Contents

I dedicate this work to

my wife, Sue,

without whose encouragement this would not have been written

and

to my son, Randy, my daughter, Virginia,

and to

my grandchildren Malia, Vincent, Joshua, and David

who were a large part of my reason for beginning.

Introduction

THE READER

This book is intended for a specific kind of reader. As I began this work, I had in mind my wife, children, and a few friends. It was my desire to equip them to take charge of their own financial future. The person to whom I have something to say is the one who has managed to acquire some savings and wishes to enhance growth and income to the extent consistent with safeguarding his or her savings. I hope to give you a conceptual framework to achieve this. The size of the savings makes little difference, it could be a hundred dollars or ten million. The principles are the same, although their application must be somewhat different. They may be applied, for example, in building up a nest egg for one's children out of $10 and $20 gifts.

I am <u>not</u> writing for the reader who will joyously risk everything if he can thereby hope to become fabulously wealthy. I am not writing for those who contemplate the sudden acquisition of inordinate wealth or plunging into excessive risk. Neither do I address experts in any investment area. Their expertise will bestow upon them opportunities denied to the rest of us, including those who buy their publicly disseminated advice.

THE BOOK

With this book I hope to provide the beginning or unsure investor with the basic guidelines to produce satisfactory investment results for his or herself. But why should there be another work on investments? Has there not already been quite enough written in the field?

I have encountered an astonishing number of misconceptions about stocks, bonds, and other investment media and about how they may be put to use. Many of these misconceptions shape investment practice, often leading people to avoid solid opportunities while unknowingly gambling recklessly. Such misconceptions are to be found even with intelligent and learned people.

Even within the community of investment analysts and counselors, there is more than just possibility of error. These professionals are a very able group, but one so small and positioned that each is subjected to an enormously reverberating influence from the prevailing climate of opinion. This makes a fertile ground for the propagation of insufficiently examined truisms.

There are many experts in the field who are extremely intelligent and have enunciated clear and valuable principles; but they are not likely to be the ones from whom you hear directly, unless you hire them as personal advisors. Furthermore, even if you did have access to them, you would probably be receiving advice on what to do today, rather than conceptual guidelines. However, you are more likely to be exposed to those who bombard you with schemes they tout or opportunities they glorify.

Many good books do exist in the field. However, the vast majority of them was written as textbooks and rarely circulate outside of classrooms. There are a few very good ones that are written for popular consumption. I will refer to and recommend two of these, those by Graham and Dreman listed in the bibliography. But there are none with which I would not find some points of contention or qualification. Furthermore, my treatment of the subject is quite different and, I believe, more helpful.

I have given the material presented here an organizational format, which I hope facilitates a broad conceptual understanding. In addition, the reader will find here contradiction to some widespread myths, as well as a glimpse at some psychological traps. As this book is written for those who do not feel fully competent in investing, it does not venture into esoteric topics like derivatives.

THE SUBJECT

Aristotle claimed moderate wealth to be conducive to the good life; a means to health, vitality, and pleasure. Above all, it bestows freedom from distractions and constraints that interfere with the exercise of our highest faculties. Thus, enhanced savings foster elevated personal freedom, allowing one to rise above the daily chores of existing to engage in pursuits deemed most meaningful. It also provides the means to satisfy one's basic needs of food, shelter, clothing, and medical care so that such burdens are not placed on others. This is the objective here: what I seek to enable the investor to secure from his savings.

Accordingly, I must speak of designing investments to be profitable. In our twenty-first century American middle-class culture, both words, *investment* and *profit*, have a shady connotation, being held somehow obscene. Much as a Victorian treated sex secretively, so the liberal American has difficulty with profit. Therefore, in beginning, I will try to dispel our stereotype. In this attempt, I will use not argument, but clarification of terms.

Investment is the purposeful expenditure of something of value (such as time, money, materials, or effort) to achieve a specifically envisioned and more valuable objective. By this definition, we would consider a student straining to master a subject or a craftsman weaving a fishing net to be investing. So too a musician composing a symphony, a businessman building a factory, or an individual buying stock or starting a savings account is investing.

Note that the envisioned objective has to be esteemed more valuable than the cost or expenditure. If this were not the case, we would be talking not of investment, but of consumption, waste, or vandalism. The increase in value successfully obtained by the investment is <u>profit</u>. Thus, Handel's fabled expenditure of twenty-four days to compose the *Messiah* was a remarkably profitable investment: the music magnificent, the cost meager. An investment may fail to achieve profit in a several ways: the objective may not be realized, the expenditure to reach it may be more valuable than the objective, or the objective proves to have unsuspected and dominant bad consequences.

However, in what follows, I will not address all investments, only the passive investments of monetary assets. For most people, these are secondary investments to enlarge the savings from their work, which is their primary investment. They are proficient with their primary investment, their lifework. In contrast, the investment of monetary assets, while almost universal in this country, is only partially familiar to most people. Therefore, some may desire further information.

Incidentally, these passive investments of monetary assets are no more worthy of contempt than are the active investments from whose savings they are made. The direct active investments are largely made possible by the passive ones generated from savings.

Passive investments are allocations of resources. All societies make them. The societal differences are in who has the right and power to make the investment decision. Is the right restricted to an elite, like a tribal chief or communist bureaucrat? Is it also granted to ordinary citizens? Can anyone who manages to save something and wishes to invest do so?

Capital is the name for the store of wealth invested to operate a productive pursuit or industry. In a nonmonetary tribal economy, canoes directed by the chief represent part of the capital of the fishing and transportation industries. Our economy is called capitalistic because capital is open to private ownership, that is, to people like you and me, acting alone or together.

The contemporary American economy may be described as security capitalism because a large part of the capital is represented by securities. These are pledges or acknowledgments of property, and their usefulness is in facilitating the transfer of small units of ownership of capital. This allows thousands of people to participate in the ownership of one enterprise. It also enables an individual to invest in small amounts.

Before moving ahead, let us note a few important propositions inherent in what has been said so far. All investment involves risk. All investment involves postponement of consumption. All investment looks to the future, which is unknowable. Thus, investments venture into the unknown, risking the fruits of past endeavors and the satisfaction of their consumption with the hope of increasing individual and societal benefits. The present work strives to give some solidity to that hope in the realm of passive investments.

In the wonderful tale of "The Emperor's New Clothes," the emperor was abased not so much by the knave who perpetrated the hoax, but most importantly by his own vanity and fears, which by shaping his beliefs, perceptions, and actions allowed him to be duped. In turn, believing in his sartorial splendor, he paraded in front of his people and, by the force of their self-doubts, led them to participate in the farce. By his lead and their adherence, the ridiculous pageantry expands to a total absurdity. In the end, an innocent lad cuts through the farce by a simple realistic observation: the Emperor is naked. With this return to reality, roars of laughter erupt, followed by the previous fantasy's legacy of mortification and disenchantment.

So it often is with investments. Dreams shaped more by deep emotional desires or aversions than by reality may predispose an investment guru or leadership group to embrace a plausible absurdity. The small investor, prey to emotions that can flame into greed or panic, distrusting his own judgment, yet needing to believe something, embraces their guidance. The presence of a following reinforces the leader's stature, in turn drawing more adherents. Such a spectacle may inflame and intoxicate with the promise of its destination, until, inevitably, the thrust of reality explodes the dream.

Hazards of this and other kinds may beset the investor. You are best prepared by knowing something of both your own possible reactions and investment realities. Fortunately, only a few simple principles will go a long way toward minimizing risk, enhancing benefits, and preserving peace of mind. You need neither become an expert nor devote great amounts of time to manage your investments well. Know yourself, your objectives, the general elements of investments, and a few strategic and tactical principles.

PART ONE

PSYCHOLOGICAL HAZARDS
AND ISSUES

Chapter 1

Psychological Hazards

MARKETS REFLECT PSYCHOLOGICAL PHENOMENA

Psychological forces shape the various markets, including those for gold, land, stocks, and bonds. Market actions are made up of decisions. People decide to buy or to sell, decide to regard a price as appropriate or inappropriate, and decide to use leverage (partially borrowed funds) or not. These investment decisions are made by human beings acting either individually or collectively. Human decisions are influenced by emotions, perceptions, biases, and understandings. It is not mere metaphor that the stock market crash of 1929 was called a "panic"; market buying is described as "frenzied"; market actions are "overreactions"; or that some investors have "faith" in their newsletter advisor, who sometimes has the "status" of a "guru."

The Myth of the Economic Man

Classical economists rested assumptions about underlying decision making on the hypothetical "economic man." This model human made rational decisions logically reached from clearly perceived and reasonably integrated objective facts. An extension of this model of clear perception and perfect rationality to the financial markets is the "efficient market" hypothesis. This holds that stock or bond prices spring from unbiased integration of known objective facts so that these prices are always about where they ought to be. Actually both hypotheses, the economic man and the efficient market, are more sophisticated than I have represented; nevertheless, they are untenable as adequate descriptions of market behavior.

If investors are so perceptive and rational, why are the onset of bear markets (those with sustained falling prices) characterized by the greatest optimism? Why are bull markets (those with sustained rising prices) immediately preceded by the greatest pessimism? Why, during the decade of the 1970s, was the best time to buy stocks in December 1974, precisely when stock's earnings and dividends were valued the least? Why do valuations of earnings and dividends of even such stodgy stocks as comprise the Dow Jones swing up and down by as much as 400%? Why do enormous pendulum-like swings in valuation suddenly and rapidly occur?

The precipitous drop and quick rebound of the valuations of Spectra-Physics' stock presents an example. Beginning in 1973, its price/earnings ratio (which is price per share divided by earnings per share and abbreviated P/E) plunged within a year from forty-three to nine, and then in just seven months rebounded to fifty-four for a 500% increase. The underlying fundamentals of earnings and dividends had no corresponding swings of that rapidity and magnitude. It seems doubtful that such instability and error are nurtured by perfection of logic, clarity of perception, or the careful weighing and integration of all the known objective facts.

Being humans, we have all had occasion to observe human decision making. Have you, dear reader, in observing the behavior of your acquaintances been aware that optimal decisions are always made and that they are reached by the unswerving application of logical reasoning founded upon uniform clarity of perception? Or perhaps there is something about economic decisions that promotes the governance of clear reason. Could it be that people reserve clear reason unalloyed with emotions just for economic matters? But then, what are we to make of economic fads like Pet Rocks, Hula-hoops, or clothing upon which the price is escalated only because of a label? Are we to assume that the "compulsive gambler" is really endowed with superior insight so that his future fortune is accurately envisioned?

Some observers of human behavior, like Freud, have portrayed humans as deeply irrational. People are seen to pursue unknown ends by means beyond their awareness. Indeed, these observers view the appearance of clear perception as coincidental and the use of logic as either superficial or in the service of a masquerade. Without going to this extreme, may we not have the temerity to doubt the universal perfection of clarity and reason in economic matters?

Irving Janis, a Yale psychologist who has devoted much study to the question of decision making, observes, " . . . The fact remains that human beings, programmed as they are with emotions and unconscious motives as well as with cognitive abilities, seldom can approximate a state of detached affectlessness when making decisions . . ."[1] Accordingly, I would like to propose the intrusion in human economic activity, and hence market behavior, of the following sources of potential hazard for market behavior.

Emotions

People invest out of anticipation of gain. The door is thus open to the pull of appetite. The possibility of large rapid gains may whet avarice. Desire may be goaded by spectacular market action and possibly incited by brokers, advisory newsletters, miscellaneous promoters, and managers whose own business depends on the number of involved clients and the volume and rapidity of activity. From the other direction, the prospect of loss may prompt fear, which if stimulated may degenerate into panic.

The investor's feelings will have their imprint on his or her actions. Feelings stemming from self-assessment are likely to be particularly influential. People whose general self-confidence is low are likely to seek out and be influenced by advice. The helpfulness of this depends upon whom they select and also upon the extent to which, in the process of receiving direction, they abandon the use of their own reason. The overconfident may undertake actions on their own without sufficient understanding of the risks being created. They may also be unaware of more promising investments.

Distortion of Perception and Reasoning

In the grip of strong emotions, what you see and think you know may be so influenced that its relation to objective, verifiable fact can become distorted, perhaps beyond any similarity. A hope nurtured with desire may mutate a wild speculation into a sure thing. An apprehension may change into an imminent catastrophe. Shakespeare put it this way:

> Such tricks hath strong imagination,
> that if it would but apprehend some joy,
> it comprehends some bringer of that joy;
> or in the night, imagining some fear,
> how easy is a bush supposed a bear![2]

In 1947, two psychologists, Brunner and Goodman,[3] performed a classic study demonstrating the impact of need and value on perception. Children of poor and affluent families were shown either coins or cardboard disks and asked to indicate their size by adjusting a variable disk of light. It was found that coins were judged to be larger than cardboard disks. Poor children judged the coins larger than the others, and all children's overestimations increased according to the value of the coin being matched. Although later studies raised questions about these findings, they nevertheless supported the view that needs and values influence memory and may be important determiners of perception in ambiguous situations.

Imagine yourself seated in darkness. A voice says that in a moment a light will appear and asks you to report what it spells out as it moves. The light appears. It moves. It's hard to make sense of the pattern. It seems erratic. You watch and ponder the elusive tracing. Then, suddenly, it's clear. In the darkness, the light has spelled out an emotionally charged word. Afterward, it is explained to you that this was an exploration of the use of the autokinetic phenomenon as a projective instrument. What you were looking at was a stationary point of light. The apparent movement is a normal illusion, which for some people may serve as an ambiguous figure that may be given form and meaning by the observer's projection or personal attribution.

Such projection of one's own feelings onto the world around us is facilitated by ambiguity. It is also facilitated by the strength of our feelings. When effects like these may be found in a situation that is both highly structured and that admits only a slender impact of needs and values, imagine what may result when fear, greed, pride, shame, or other passions are aroused in the more amorphous domain of investments.

In day-to-day situations, novelists, salesmen, orators, confidence men, as well as psychologists are aware of some of the influences that can erode rational judgment. It behooves us to be aware of some of these influences, especially those to which we personally are most susceptible so that we can minimize or compensate for their corrosive effect on our decisions. Let us briefly note some dynamisms having importance for investment, which may orient the passions to interfere with rational assessment and judgment.

Selective Attention

From out of the enormous array of stimuli impinging upon us, we have learned to impose order by selecting some key elements and ignoring the rest. We have learned this so well that we are essentially unaware that we continually make selections. It is appropriate that we do this. Otherwise we could not act. However, the more familiar we are with an area, the more we shape what we perceive to accord with (a) what we have already learned, that is, our concepts and opinions, and (b) what is important to us, that is, our values. Perhaps this is one of the reasons why youth is a time of greater curiosity and freshness of interest. As we gather experience, things have a tendency to become more repetitious and predictable. We are more and more witnesses to a confirmation of our opinions; that is, unless something shocks us away from their sufficiency. Thus in making a decision, whether for an investment or other purpose, even though we may have been surrounded by all the pertinent facts, we may remain blissfully unaware of conclusive elements.

Once having ventured a position, we will be prone to see confirmation and discount invalidation. The tendency toward confirmation is enhanced further by defense of one's conceptual system described below. We are likely to interpret something ambiguous as confirmation. Even a simple restatement may be construed as additional confirmation. Thus, starting from an idea that the market is rising, we may be led to transform this into a conviction that it will and must continue to rise. If we start with the notion that stock ownership is precariously risky, we may incline to push ourselves into inflexible avoidance. Selective attention, therefore, predisposes people toward prematurely fixed opinions, that is, toward dogmatism. Although this may be more distressing in other areas of life, the investor is faced with a field in which risk is latent at every turn. Dogmatic certainty in this setting predisposes one toward lost opportunities and needless risks.

Nevertheless, should contrary evidence or opinion attack with enough strength or persistence to smash through our defensive screen, revision will be required. If this happens quickly, we can luckily retain flexibility. The longer this takes, the stronger must the contrary evidence have to be to have an impact. In that case, we are apt to swing from uncritical acceptance of a position to uncritical rejection. As a bull market nears its top and characteristic ebullient optimism boils up in the press, TV, and conversations, the person who has been too cautious to invest in stocks is now finally ready to convert by the overwhelming public "validation." Ironically, this is when the risk has indeed mounted to a crescendo, leaving the investor at the edge of a precipice from which an ultimate fall will reinvigorate the original prejudice with a new tenacity.

The Halo Effect

Psychologists collided with a barrier when they began to construct rating scales of distinct individual traits. This was the "halo effect," which blurs the pattern of distinct traits. Cronbach[4] explains that "the observer forms a general opinion about the person's merit, and his ratings of specific traits are strongly influenced by the overall impression." This influence is demonstrated by strong positive correlations between traits no matter how independent one would suppose they really are. Although this halo effect was found in the context of rating individuals, where there may be motivation for boosting one person's ratings and depressing another's, it is also strongly suggestive that many people tend to judge by making a simple overall evaluative judgment (for example: this is a good guy or a bad guy; this is a good stock or a bad stock; stocks are good or bad) and then view everything else about the person or thing through this point of view.

An evaluative bias can spring from several sources. Some arise from personal associations like it's the first investment one ever made, your father gave you the stock, or its name sounds comforting. You may have come to accept an image projected by the company or its critics. Thus, one's judgments may be influenced by initial evaluative prejudices. Such a pattern can seriously interfere with a sufficient appraisal of the merits. Putting aside the havoc this could wreak in other areas of life, regarding investments, it can push one into uncritically taking positions. Being swayed by an irrelevant bias, one may then reject, acquire, or hold issues or forms of investment without due regard to their suitability.

The Hazard of Unidimensional Thinking

It has been hypothesized by Kelly[5] that before any action can be undertaken, all relevant information and issues must be constricted to a single dimension so that a simple yes or no decision can be made. Ideally, one begins by thinking of all necessary information that, even in the relatively simple area of investments, is complex and multidimensional. But since one cannot "mount his horse and ride off in all directions,"[6] one reduces everything to a single dimension to fit the requirements of action, which is either go or no-go. Ideally after deciding, one should then embrace again the whole complex picture as a basis for future thinking.

This is an inescapable requirement for action, that however complex the problem, everything must be broken down to a yes or no, a simple bipolar unidimensional judgment. This poses a critical danger point. A good decision requires that the final single dimension upon which the decision will be made must be adequately representative of the entire multidimensional realm. Observation of decision making suggests that this is unusual. Sometimes, disappointingly, after a thorough analysis of relevant factors, a decision is made by simply leaping to the most salient, favored, or persuasive of the several dimensions and putting aside the rest.

Sometimes one may short-circuit the decision-making process by leaving aside the initial multidimensional analysis entirely. If one is blessed with having selected a crucial dimension, everything may proceed smoothly. However, even if one has a flair for selecting the one critical dimension, this is a hazardous procedure, favored by some of the more spectacular blunderers. The investment strategy outlined later in this book includes one simple method to ensure the appropriateness of the final single dimension upon which a decision will be reached. One can use a decision-making dimension that is made of and is an index for several of the most critical requirements.

Conformity

Using the autokinetic phenomenon mentioned above, Sherif[7] found that individuals asked to estimate the distance the actually stationary light moved developed their own individual norms, characteristic for the individual but differing widely from person to person. Having individuals for whom stable characteristic norms had been established in individual sessions placed together in groups of two or three, Sherif found that when expressed in the group, judgments converged. Brown,[8] summarizing a number of studies on conformity in subjective judgment situations, concludes, "There seems to be an almost ineradicable tendency for members of a group to move toward agreement. It occurs when there is no instruction to reach a consensus. It occurs when there is no opportunity to argue. It even occurs, incipiently, when the members do not know one another's opinions but can only guess at them."

Asch,[9] in a classic series of studies on conformity in reporting objective situations, used confederate subjects (stooges) to pit one person's clear and obvious judgment of physical reality against the unanimous pronouncements of a contradictory group. Approximately one of three judgments conformed to the group judgment and violated clearly-sensed reality. When faced with contradictory group judgments, subjects' physiological indices indicated sharp anxiety. Agreement with the group tended to reduce anxiety. However, anxiety remained high for those rendering independent judgments.

What relevance does this potent conformity have to investments and particularly to the erosion of judgment in making investment decisions? The relation is twofold. One aspect is relatively obvious and straightforward. The other is somewhat more subtle and insidious in that it is an important part of a loop between the investor and his advisors whereby <u>the advisors in leading the investor are following</u>, but let's postpone this to the next chapter.

The obvious relationship is magnified by the investor's sense of his own limited competence in a field that is supposed to be complex and dominated by experts. An obvious solution therefore is to find an expert. A corollary of this solution, given the expert's supposed mastery and the investor's supposed incompetence, is the suspension of one's own judgment. Conformity leads one to become susceptible to what others say regardless of its merit. The "expert" opinions may come from tips from friends, newspaper articles, magazines, or television. More systematic but also questionable advice may come from investment newsletters and brokers. Skilled and astute investment counselors do not press their attentions upon the small investor so conspicuously. They tend to be overlooked or prohibitively expensive. The pressure of conformity, therefore, predisposes one to abandon the use of one's own learning and judgment and instead substitute judgment that may or may not be helpful and whose motivations may not always steer the advice in the investor's best interest.

The investment community may be characterized as having a number of major opinion makers who are (1) relatively few in number and (2) generally aware of what each other is saying. Albeit to a much lesser degree, pressures of conformity operate, and a climate of opinion tends to develop about the economy, about future trends, and about the relative merits of alternative investment media. One result is that many people will tend to be doing the same things at about the same time. This predisposes markets to overreaction. Furthermore, by slavishly following advice, the conforming small investor is likely to be doing substantially what the others are doing, but <u>significantly later</u>. Prices will have moved up before he has bought and down before he has sold. For the conforming investor, market overreactions will not be opportunities; they will be traps. His chances of buying when prices are too high, of selling when prices are low, and of refraining from acting when prices are advantageous are increased.

Another disadvantage of conforming to many brokers and advisory newsletters is their short-term trading orientation. This predisposition may be fostered by (1) commissions being increased by frequency of transactions and (2) quick results being more alluring and spectacular. As we shall see, frequency of transactions enlarges the toll of commissions and taxes, which damages ultimate results. Furthermore, contrary to expectation, a short-term outlook encourages one to venture onto the least predictable terrain.

Conceptual System Defense

George Kelly, in expounding one of the most penetrating and comprehensive of psychological theories,[5] portrays each human as constructing and elaborating a distinct individual conceptual system in order to understand and influence the world about him. It is the individual who "erects his own alternative approaches to reality."[10] The things one tries to understand do not force their reality upon the observer, except by being consistent or inconsistent with the observer's expectations. These expectations may be thought of as informal predictions.

One's conceptual system is thus one's own construction. It is a theoretical structure built by the individual after countless successive interactions. Its preservation and elaboration, especially concerning its central or core governing concepts, is of major importance to the individual. (Not only is it one's often painfully-acquired system; but without it, one would be deprived of understanding.) Finding oneself in a situation where one's central beliefs are either invalidated or do not apply is devastating. Being caught with one's constructs down is to be naked, vulnerable, and without resource. The defense and adjustment of one's conceptual system is crucial.

The impact that an incompatible observation will have upon one's conceptual system will depend upon that system. If disconfirmation results in an adjustment of one's conceptual system whereby it becomes a better predictor, then the disconfirmation has been beneficial. This is, however, not the only possible response. One of the important determinants of response is the degree of flexibility of the higher level or more abstract concepts. Rigid systems, those that cannot smoothly admit and integrate new information, call for more drastic measures to protect the ideational status quo. One may do a number of things to save one's belief system in the face of disconfirmation. For example, the disconfirmation may be rejected, reinterpreted to be confirmation, or redefined to be irrelevant.

Within the sphere of investments, this kind of distortion of rational processes is most likely to hit the individual investor indirectly through its effect on investment gurus. Typically the investor's concern with investments is incidental (he has only money at stake) and, therefore, from Kelly's perspective, would not be likely to use such a rigid defense. A professional advisor, however, operating either through his own theory or one toward which he has made a professional affiliation, has much more at stake. An invalidation of the theory that he has publicly propounded and touted must involve his concept of himself as a competent professional. That is a powerful reason for a theoretical defense so staunch as to sidestep logical requirements. Rokeach referred to extreme conceptual system defense as "closed-mindedness" and observed, "The more closed the belief system, the more is the acceptance of a particular belief assumed to depend on irrelevant internal drives and/or arbitrary reinforcements from external authority . . . the more open the system, the more should the person address himself to objective structural requirements . . ."[11]

Looking at some theoretical systems operative in the investment world suggests that the kind of closed-minded defense envisioned here is embodied by a number of Wall Street pundits. Several theories used as platforms from which to peddle advice are reminiscent of Rokeach's description: they are short on objective demonstration while being long on obvious personal need for maintenance. Unfounded systems have been used professionally to predict market actions. As examples of the predictors to which some professionals cling and their related defensive reasoning, let's just take a peek at two of them: the January Indicator and the Kondratieff Wave theory.

The January Indicator

Hulbert's critique of <u>the January Indicator</u>, the ensuing defensive objections, and his subsequent demonstration of invalidity[12] present an excellent disclosure of the professional use of an invalidated hypothesis together with a defensive reaction sidestepping objective logical observation. The indicator, which a number of advisory newsletters use, is simply that as the market goes in January, so it will go for the year. Of the newsletter editors touting the indicator, Hulbert quotes one who wrote, "The January Barometer . . . is well respected. It . . . sports an 85% 'guarantee' that the full year will reflect the direction of its first month." Implying that its greatest strength was in detecting important market declines, the editor went on to say, "It's a great bear-catcher."[13]

The 85% "guarantee" was apparently derived from the observation that in the preceding six years, the relationship held in five and failed in one year (which is 83.3% of the time). In looking over the data, Hulbert could find no other reason for the percentage of "guarantee." For the moment, let us leave aside Hulbert's analysis and just look at what is being propounded because it is an <u>utterly false kind of representation frequently repeated in investment circles</u>. The simple percentage observed is being confused with the efficiency of prediction! <u>Before leaping to an assertion of how efficient our predictor is, we must first determine whether we have a predictor at all</u>!

If we look at any large array of number relationships, we will see all kinds of things. Let us assume we have walked into a Los Vegas casino and see a roulette wheel. We watch three times and see that each time, red comes up. Do we come up with the silly conclusion that red comes up 100% of the time and is therefore a guarantee with which we should ride? Yet that's precisely the kind of reasoning used by the newsletter editor. Instead, the first thing we want to do if we are looking for a predictor is to see if we have one. Therefore, we must first rule out the possibility that what we have observed arose merely by chance. For, if it is a chance result, it will predict nothing with validity, no matter how good it looked. Even a 100% finding is meaningless if we cannot confidently reject the idea that it arose from chance. In this case, we determine the chance probability at eighteen red squares out of a total of thirty-eight squares, or eighteen divided by thirty-eight, or .47 for one occurrence. For the two successive occurrences, we square this number and arrive at .22. Now, we do not really have three successive predicted occurrences. The first time could have been anything, what counts is only that the second and third agreed with the first. We may therefore state the observed probability of three reds in succession at twenty-two times out of one hundred. Clearly, here the likelihood of getting the observed result is so high that we have no grounds to discard the hypothesis of a chance finding. Thus, far from having a predictor with 100% effectiveness, we have no predictor at all.

Returning to "the January Indicator," if we look at the probability of five years out of six in which the rest of the year mirrors January, the result is given by the binomial expansion at .1093 or eleven times in a hundred. We cannot reject with any confidence the possibility that this was merely a chance occurrence. The possibility of a chance occurrence is simply too large. <u>Therefore, far from having a predictor with 85% effectiveness, we have no predictor at all</u>.

Hulbert took a broader look at the January Indicator. He looked at the preceding seventy years (1916-1986) and found that in 64% of the years, January correctly predicted the rest of the year. (Incidentally, the odds on this happening by chance are 28.5 times out of 100, I would therefore reject this out of hand as a predictor; it is way above the customary <u>minimal confidence standards</u> of less than 5 or 1% likelihood of being a chance finding. We therefore have no grounds for confidence that a predictive relationship exists. Furthermore, a hypothesis derived, as this presumably was, by an <u>arbitrary</u> search through a wide number of variables demands a correspondingly more stringent confidence level. This is because a blind search through a large number of variables increases the possibility of a chance finding.)

Hulbert then goes on to compare two alternate hypothetical investments of $10,000 in the stocks of the Dow Jones index. Following the January Indicator, he calculated the results of buying each year in which January was up, and selling stocks short after a January decline. This was compared to simply buying the stocks in 1916 and holding them. Following the January Indicator resulted in the $10,000 appreciating to $11,955 across the seventy years. This is less than two-tenths of 1% per year. Meanwhile, the comparison of merely buying and holding appreciated from $10,000 to $155,993. So much for being a great "bear-catcher."

Defensive Rebuttals

Hulbert received three kinds of objections.[12] First, there was a quibble over the definition of the *year*. Hulbert applied the indicator to the rest of the calendar year, that is, from February 1 through December 31. One objection was that there was no reason to be out of the market in January so that the following twelve months should be used. The reader will note that the definition was changed after invalidation. However, the revised definition casts even greater doubt on the indicator, for the correspondence rate drops from 64% to 58%.

The second objection was that Hulbert should not have sold the stock short when the indicator predicted a down year. One may wonder why this objection is posed when the indicator is supposed to predict a down year and it is said to be especially good at being a "bear-catcher." A third objection raised was that the indicator should only be used after the midthirties due to the economic and monetary developments of that time. Note that this objection raises two new conditions that would rule out of consideration the least validating stretch of years. The removal of invalidating data after a negative finding may be appropriate for something regarded as a tentative hypothesis for which refinement is sought. However, it is at best a suspect procedure for something put forward as an established position by "professionals." Note, also, that the introduction of the idea of relatedness to economic and monetary conditions essentially undermines its role as a useful predictor, for economic and monetary conditions are always subject to unknown change during the course of any year.

My comments above are meant only to highlight the bias behind the objections. Hulbert provides their empirical demolition. He accommodated to the objections by making new calculations with the revised assumptions. The January Indicator still failed by large margins to match a simple buy-and-hold strategy. Neither beginning in 1935, redefining the rest of the year, nor avoiding short sales, can overcome the large advantage of a simple buy-and-hold. Using the indicator would have resulted in money lost. Its lack of corroboration has been sidestepped by some who continue its uses.

The Kondratieff Wave

In the 1920s, a Russian economist, Nikolai Kondratieff, observed that "the western world had experienced two and a half long economic cycles since the end of the eighteenth century, each lasting approximately fifty years."[14] He related these to rising commodity prices approximately coincident with major wars followed by later price declines. I have no wish to impugn Kondratieff who consummated an apparently exhaustive and insightful study. Nor would I assail anyone's drawing hypotheses from his work. The relation between wars and commodity prices has both good evidence and rationale.

However, let's briefly consider what investment experts did when they called upon the fifty-year Kondratieff Wave to advocate liquidation of security positions in the 1970s. Note that in the 1920s when his wave was propounded, its status was merely a hypothesis with no more claim to validity than any hypothesis you or I might dream up. Why, you might ask, should it be denied a higher status? Because it was derived from a search through historical records to see what patterns could be found. When this is done broadly enough, many patterns are available to be seen, and while some may reflect enduring relationships, others are merely coincidental. Thus, having found the pattern by a wide-ranging record search, one has a hypothesis that, if it is to be applied as a predictor, must first be validated. This is done by seeing how well it predicts <u>after its formulation</u>. At the time it was being touted, it had not yet had time to go through one cycle. There were at best two points of approximately accurate intersect with subsequent observation: the crash of the late twenties and the rise of the sixties. Two approximately congruent points do not make a validation. Furthermore, when applied to stock prices, the two-point correspondence really seems to distort the picture of what was happening. Rather than a large swing down followed by an equivalent large upward swing as in a wave, if one looks at the Value Line Index of stock prices, one sees an essentially continuously rising pattern from the mid-1930s to the present. What we have then at the most is an interesting hypothesis with some validating evidence, but by no means sufficient support to justify "professional" use as a predictor.

MARKETS ALSO REFLECT OBJECTIVE VALUES

Having disparaged the "economic man" as a myth, it must now be partially resurrected. It is not totally false. It errs only in its version of untempered extremity.

The Myth of the Irrational Man

There is a model that holds humankind to be essentially irrational. The facts contradict it. It can claim even less justification than the economic man. Much of what seems to be irrationality is the observer's ignorance of the motives involved. If we assume a person to be trying to do one thing when he is really trying to do something quite different, we may prematurely and wrongly conclude that he is irrational. If by chance we discover his different motive, we then may prematurely and wrongly conclude that he holds that motive irrationally because we are not privy to his view of the world. Much that even psychotic people do is understandable and even logical when viewed from their perspective of the situation confronting them. Patients sometimes describe the entrance into a psychotic state itself as the result of a logical decision. Finding no superior alternative solution to the impossible and noxious reality confronting them, they occasionally report having decided on a complete withdrawal. Many psychologists indeed view problematic behavior as having emerged as an appropriate adaptation to a deviant situation. The misfit appears when the person perpetuates what was learned in one peculiar situation where it was appropriate into another situation where it is inappropriate. Thus, much of what we call bizarre behavior springs rationally from a different interpretation of the situation.

Even Freud, and other psychoanalysts who have portrayed humans as irrational, caution that to properly understand a person's situation, one must never overlook "secondary gain." "Secondary gain" refers to the obvious realistic benefits that the patient's condition obtains. This may include insurance proceeds, sympathy, support, etc.

The author engaged in a clinical study of chronic psychiatric patients in which the behavior of nursing and paramedical staff toward each patient was analyzed for its relationship to the patient's key problem in living. Where such a relationship was thought to worsen the patient's problem, an attempt was made to alter the behavior of the staff to promote appropriate rather than dysfunctional behavior by the patients.[15] The problem of one patient, code named John, is a good example of the problem being a good adaptation to the situation.

John, a twenty-eight-year-old man, had been hospitalized continuously for seven years with no improvement and a dismal prognosis. John spent most days in bed pouting or crying, frequently with the covers pulled over his head, and refusing to engage in activities, including going to meals. John appeared to thrive on kindly attention and recognition as a "man." It was found that when he had his regressive episodes, the response by staff was to go to his bedside, lavish him with attention, assuage his injured feelings, and coax him to resume activities. Of course, when John had a good day, the staff, having time to attend to other priorities, neglected him. Under the hypothesis that the kindly attention and recognition were rewards that, however unintentionally, did actually support his disability, the staff was urged to reverse their rewards. That is, they were to give him the freedom to cry in bed as much as he wished. The attention, empathy, and recognition were to be in response to John's venturing out of bed, not to his crying. Because of excellent initial results, pouting by itself was added as something not to reward.

The nursing staff's report on John summarized, " . . . Remarkable progress. In the past four months he has had only one regressive episode, and it was brief and mild. He is now maintaining paid employment. Each day he now lives with stresses far greater than those that use to provoke his episodes."[15] Could it not be argued that John's previously disordered behavior had been a rational response to a disordered situation?

Nevertheless, the best indication that most behavior is rational comes from its correspondence to objectively verifiable facts. In the realm of investments, there is a plethora of such evidence attesting to rational behavior. For example, look at the ratio of price to earnings (P/E). The mere existence of such a ratio shows that at least some people are interested in relating the cost of a stock to its earnings, which is a fundamental and objective index of value. Although there is some room for accounting judgment in deriving a figure for earnings, it may be said to be objective because it is derived by standard procedures from observable facts.

Going beyond the mere existence of the P/E ratio, there exist rules of thumb about what constitutes acceptable ratios in general, for an industry, or for a particular company. These rules of thumb imply price ranges to be normal, bargains, or excessive. Furthermore, over long periods of time, stocks fluctuate around these normative values, so that departures from the norms suggest eventual correction.

The markets sustain appropriate mathematical relations between different values. For example, as the date of conversion of a preferred stock into the company's common stock approaches, the price of the preferred will approach the price of the common adjusted by the exchange ratio. Indeed, there are people known as arbitrageurs who make a living by looking for any inconsistencies between related issues and markets and, if they find discrepancies, making simultaneous purchases in the cheaper and sales in the more expensive. Their actions provide the unintentional service of keeping markets in tandem around the world. Their existence as well as their accomplishments evince rationality in markets.

MARKETS REFLECT BIASED AND FALLIBLE ATTEMPTS AT OBJECTIVITY

I propose that we view the markets as made up of transactions by a composite of investors who differ as regards rationality and objectivity not only from each other, but also within themselves across time. To describe the general investment tendency of this composite, I further propose that we merge the two models of the "economic man" and the "irrational man," preserving something from each. From the "economic man," let us preserve the thrust toward rationality and objective perception, but let us jettison the notion of perfection and reliability of functioning. From the "irrational man," let us preserve the recognition that psychological biases may cloud clarity of perception and at times promote apparently impulsive, dysfunctional behavior; but let us discard the concept that all judgments are irrational and that there is no connection to objective reality.

Let us keep in mind both aspects of the quotation from Irving Janis given at the outset: " . . . The fact remains that human beings, programmed as they are with emotions and unconscious motives as well as with cognitive abilities, seldom can approximate a state of detached affectlessness when making decisions . . ." (emphasis added).[1] The investor may wish to gain greater awareness of his or her own propensities and the directions in which they are inclined to push. I hope the investor may find in this book perspectives and strategies through which undesired results may be avoided or mitigated. I also hope that the investor may become aware of the overreactions of the market and benefit rather than be trapped by them. The first advice to an investor is to know yourself, your predispositions, values, goals, time horizon, and tolerance for risk.

The second advice is to see the market as a result of the changing interplay of rational, reality-linked forces together with such forces as ego involvement, greed, fear, and impatience. We may therefore expect what is customarily seen across a wide expanse of time, which is that in the long run, relatively realistic norms prevail as a central tendency about which upward or downward distortions occur. In the short run, almost anything can happen. When distortions occur, eventually corrections follow. The more severe or prolonged the distortion, the more robust will be the following correction. It should of course be recognized that a "correction" may usher in a new distortion.

Chapter 2

Your Leader May Be Following You

YOU DETERMINE THE INVESTMENT AUTHORITIES

If you lack confidence in your ability to superintend your investments, you may want someone to guide you. Regardless of how that person comes to your attention, you select your investment advisor and determine how the advisory relationship will proceed—if only by acquiescence. You do this by agreeing to listen or to pay the requested fees. Not only do you determine who your particular advisors are, but collectively with the vast population of investors, you bestow status and authority upon the investment pundits. They achieve their status by appealing successfully to you.

This is a facet of the citizen's role in a democratic and partially capitalistic country. We elect our political leaders, choose our doctors, and collectively decide what goods shall be produced and in what quantities. With our investment advisors, however, our ignorance may lead us somewhat more astray. The criteria for selection of political leaders are simpler and more visible. The primary criterion is that they advocate those of our wishes that do not infringe upon the rights of others, since being responsive to the people is their charge. For doctors and lawyers, the primary standard is likely to be competence; here we are helped by established boards who examine and certify to at least a minimum competence. When buying an automobile, we may view its lines, settle into the driver's seat, submit it to a test-drive, and at our leisure, consider how it will meet our requirements.

We may want an investment advisor because we feel unknowing. How then, from the quagmire of that ignorance, do we find a solid base to establish a choice where almost nothing is tangible or certified? Can we recognize true expertise that will be honestly placed at the service of the <u>client's</u> long-term interest? Are we clear about what standards to apply?

THE LEADER IS CHOSEN BY CONFORMING TO THE FOLLOWERS

How does a hopeful advisor prompt a favorable selection? The selection may be viewed as a special and circumscribed case of leadership determination. Bales[1] finds leadership to emerge from three basic dimensions: <u>activity</u>, <u>task ability</u>, and <u>likability</u>. Transferring these to the quest of the prospective investment advisor, activity may involve promotional outreach and frequency of trades. Task ability reflects an image compounded of historical results, seductive promises, and endorsements, usually indirect. The importance of likability undoubtedly depends upon the closeness of the advisory relation—for a broker much more important than for a newsletter editor.

But who weighs these three dimensions, and what standards are applied to arrive at a decision? Reviewing studies on small groups, Brown[2] observes, "We have come upon a central paradox of social leadership . . . the leader is the member who most fully lives up to the norms of the group . . . The leader accepts the central values of the group . . ." But does the group or the leader impose the norms and values? Efforts to answer this question suggest that there is an interaction of influence between the leader and the group in shaping the group's position, but that the group probably sets the limits or context permitting the leader's influence to operate. For all of his reputedly mesmerizing persuasiveness, it is nevertheless doubtful that a Hitler could reasonably aspire to be chief of state of Israel.

Your Advisor May Be Following You

The advisor, therefore, tailors his programs, goals, and statements to what he believes his prospective clientele wish. If he is to advise you individually or to act on your behalf, then by discussion you and he may work out an optimal adjustment between opposing desires as well as between fantasy and reality. If, however, he is dealing with clients in mass, such as for example, an advisory newsletter editor, his image of what is wanted may be hitched to his stereotype of the broadest spectrum of desires. He is likely to suppose that you want (1) a flood of riches with (2) immediate delivery. He may very well send you a flyer like one I received stating that "if your answer is 'no' then you may have lost out on a 723% return on your money that you could have made by buying Canadian dollar puts . . ." This flyer went on with an allusion to a "silver spread that brought investors a 100% profit . . . in a matter of months . . ."[3]

To the extent that people accept the sales pitch, they confirm the advisor's preconception of their desires. Thus, the public by its pattern of attention and inattention determines what general guidelines it will allow its expert advisors to use. <u>Therefore, such advice is often governed more by fantasy than by expertise</u>. Furthermore, because of the exigencies of good salesmanship, the desires expressed may not be the public's most important desires—merely the most ensnaring.

Pressure toward Inappropriate Activity

After being attracted, a client must be kept. As Bales notes, the first requisite is activity. As illustration, some can recall that Eisenhower was criticized most for the frequency of his golf; the implicit admonition being that he should have unflaggingly guided the ship of state. A newsletter editor who repeatedly advises, "Our course remains optimal; make no changes," is in danger of losing clients, however astute such advice may be. With pressure to live up to the role, there may be a predisposition toward frequent transactions and a short-term perspective.

Untested Ability

How accurately do we gauge Bales's second dimension, task ability? May we not sometimes trap ourselves by the spurious appearance of correctness and shun accuracy because it is unexciting? Let's suppose we have three seers: Tom, Dick, and Harry to whom as candidates for resident seer, we have given the task of predicting the flip of a coin. Tom proclaims, "Heads." Dick predicts, "Tails." Harry says, "It's a matter of probabilities which are .5 for heads and .5 for tails, so just take your choice." The flip is made, and let us suppose, it is tails. Tom, being wrong, obviously does not know what he is talking about; he is dismissed. Harry is not decisive. He fails to give unequivocal prediction, so he too is dismissed. We decide to go with Dick; he is decisive, concise, and right.

Clearly, this is an overstatement; people do not really decide like that. Nevertheless, I suggest that although it may be an illustrative exaggeration, it contains some truth about the selection of investment experts. It is true in that an expert's success or failure is frequently judged on data so limited that we cannot say the results have sprung not from ability but from chance. Sometimes we are urged to note that a potential advisor had the best record over the last year or quarter. The selection of an advisor more properly looks to what the <u>long-term</u> record (across rising and falling markets) indicates regarding ability.

Pressure toward Inappropriate Tactics

In the illustratively exaggerated example above, a few more grains of truth are contained. It is true in that the dramatic is favored over the prosaic. It is true in that the simple is preferred to the complex. While past success, drama, and simplicity may be admirable in their place, they do not necessarily lead to accurate prediction. Such prediction is more likely to come from a thorough, if prosaic, regard of fundamentals and an acknowledgment of ambiguity, however this may erode concision and drama.

If we select our advisor and influence what he tells us, to what extent have we really replaced uncertainty with expertise? May we not get some of our own frailty reflected back to us in the guise of authority? This is likely to depend upon how we select our advisor and the degree of mutual understanding about priorities.

Chapter 3

Personal Issues: Snags and Choices

<u>SNAGS</u>

<u>Common Investment Misperceptions</u>

Good as Gold

Gold has been used as a medium of exchange and as a backing for other media for so long that it has become imbued with an aura of intrinsic value. It has such a semblance of inherent value that many people were shocked in the early 1970s when the United States government severed the connection between gold and the dollar. Believing that the connection with gold is what gave the dollar its value, several pontificated on an impending currency disaster. While it is true that the currency has been pummeled, the source has been quite different.

Those who were alarmed overlooked two truths. First, the value of the dollar did not come from its link with gold, but from everybody accepting the dollar as a standard of exchange. While in the dollar's inception the link with gold may have facilitated the adoption of this convention, the convention was sustained not by gold so much as by a combination of fiat, convenience, and lack of a better alternative. Second, while gold as a metal does have some market value deriving from its usefulness, this is far too little to sustain its current price. Rather, its value, like paper money, rests primarily upon a convention of acceptance.

Samuelson, the noted author of economics textbooks, writing when the dollar was still linked to gold, said, "The modern student need not be misled, as were earlier generations of students, by some mystical belief that 'gold backing' is what gives money its value . . . Every expert knows that the popular conception 'money has more value if it is exchangeable into gold' exactly reverses the true relation. If it were not that gold has some monetary uses, its value as a metal would be much less than it is today."[1] Then, when gold and the dollar were cut loose from each other, many under the misconception that gold gave money its value chose gold rather than the dollar. The effect of its former real monetary use has been replaced by the illusion that it is a super money. Only from that arbitrary belief will gold have special support.

Originally, gold's value came from its minimal chemical reactivity, making it appropriate for dentistry, eating and drinking utensils, and adornment. Plastic, porcelain, stainless steel, etc., have been developed with even less chemical reactivity. With the speculation in gold in the late seventies, dentists intensified their work with substitute materials and now have satisfactory alternative alloys.

Currently gold's most extensive "usefulness" is in jewelry, especially the gold chains, coins, and other exhibitions that pass for adornment. Although gold has always been used in jewelry, its use was subdued and relegated to background. With the speculative price rise of gold suddenly it changed to flashy demonstration. Thorstein Veblen[2] derided this as conspicuous consumption, the public waste of value to display "power and status." However, self-confident people with indisputable power, wealth, or inner strength have no need for such symbols. Therefore, in time the meaning of the display undergoes a subtle inversion. Thus such customs are fleeting. Tomorrow's styles may serve different standards, perhaps even beauty will be pursued. What would then happen to this remaining support for the price of gold?

In summary, gold's price rests upon two shaky pillars that lift it higher than would be warranted by its use as a metal. One is the illusory aura of super money status. The other is a current jewelry fad. People relying upon these pillars may have luck, but they will need it.

Have You a Good Tip?

Some people seem to believe that the world is divided into those who know and those who are ignorant. When investing, the way of the former is to fortune while that of the latter is to misfortune. Momentary admission to the elite circle comes with the right tip. Tip is knowledge, knowledge tip, that is all you know on earth and all you need to know.

It is true that some people have inside knowledge that others do not. A company president or controller may know of some development that will soon bring triumph or disaster. Yet three barriers—ethical, legal, and practical—stand between this and an investment windfall. The ethical and legal barriers tripped Ivan Boesky and his confreres into public infamy. The practical barrier, operating for the layman, is that a tip may work more forcibly to your disadvantage than to your advantage.

Three dynamics join to produce this detrimental effect. First, the tip may be wrong. Some people treat a hypothesis or hunch as fact. Some like to be thought knowledgeable. Some will give you a boulder of conjecture to embellish their nugget of fact.

Second, and much less obvious, you may lose money even with an accurate tip. If you as a layman have received a tip, you may expect that many others before you have received the same information. For example, suppose that the information is about a disaster that has not yet been announced. Learning of this unknown disaster, many will have immediately sold the stock short. The price may thus already have been driven excessively downward before you have had a chance to act. If you sell short now, you stand the decided risk that, when the disaster is publicly announced, the stock will <u>rise</u> rather than fall! Why should it rise in response to a disaster? Because all those previous short sellers will choose this time to cover their short positions. That is, they will now buy, putting an upward pressure on the stock price. The market's response may appear quixotic to those who overlook the possibility that many people will have already acted in anticipation of events, whether by inside knowledge or deduction. This is part of the reason for the old market adage "sell on good news, buy on bad."

Third, the more you use tips, the more you destroy a coherent investment strategy. Your portfolio will jump around according to the whimsy of your contacts with tipsters. If you are a potential tip seeker, clarifying a strategy for yourself may be extremely helpful. The chapter on strategy may provide you with important anchor points.

Another Record? Absolutely!

Some people say that the stock market has never been so high. Even in the heady days in 1929 before the great crash, the Dow Jones Industrial Average was only at 380. Now it is far higher; how can this be justified? Or have you heard people amazed that "it went up another 100 points today! It never used to gain so much."

These people have fallen into the fallacy of regarding the numbers absolutely rather than relating them to an appropriate base. At 380, a 100-point jump would have meant 26.3%. At 2,600 it was reduced to 3.8%, and at 9,000 it is a measly 1.1%. Today's 100-point fluctuation is not yesterday's. Likewise comparing the height of the Dow's current level to its 1929 high of 380 (or any previous level) makes no sense without reference to their respective earnings. The extremity of a market is better judged by its average P/E ratio or dividend yield than by the absolute level of stock prices.

Stocks Are for Gambling!

Investment risks are widely misperceived: overrated and underrated. Stocks are frequently believed to be too risky for prudent investment. Some think putting one's children's savings into stocks is indistinguishable from throwing it directly onto a roulette table. While it is true that stocks present risk, their total risk when handled prudently is not appreciably greater than the total risk of other methods of saving. Indeed, in this century, well-chosen stocks have been less risky than bonds, savings accounts, or storing cash in the mattress.

Those who have lost money or seen friends lose in the stock market may take comfort in blaming stocks. To conclude that the problem lay with how one handled them or allowed them to be handled is more personal and less soothing. But mastery begins with a willingness to face reality. For those who disregard concepts of value or strategies of risk control, danger lurks around every corner, and not only in the stock market.

Another path toward overestimating the risk in stocks arises from what I call the old banker's tradition, which accords great weight to priority of claim on income and assets. While priority of claim does reduce risk, it is a relatively minor reduction from the whole spectrum of risk. Another reason I associate this view with bankers is that their work environment considers primarily the relationship between money and money. Unlike the ordinary saver who must give more weight to the relationship between money and food or medical care, the banker planning the bank's investments can remain much more comfortably oblivious to the risk of deteriorating purchasing power. As the bank's assets fall, so do its liabilities.

Hedge Inflation with Gold

Almost everyone "knows" that gold is a hedge against inflation; but this bit of lore does not pass inspection. The belief that gold is a hedge against inflation is <u>not</u> true. How can I say this when almost everyone, some authorities included, maintain the opposite, that it is a hedge. One may be comfortable departing from authority when an empirical test of reality provides the basis for the departure. If you want to know how many teeth your dog has, looking in his mouth is a much better guide than soliciting the advice of "toothsayers," who, I venture, will flock to your door if the price is right. Therefore, I invite you to look into the dog's mouth. In this day of widespread access to computers, it is not great problem.

When you correlate the yearly rises and falls of the price of gold with those of inflation over the period since the destruction of its linkage with the dollar, the result you will find is a correlation of zero. That is, no relationship between gold and inflation is found. With no relationship, you have no hedge. It is true we do not have enough time to test adequately the significance of the lack of relationship. However, if we are to use a hedge, we must want it to be strong enough to be effective. If after these years we have no trace of a relationship, we are better off looking elsewhere for a hedge.

Benefit Blindness

Investment benefits are commonly misperceived. Some are taken in by the illusion of benefits while others may disbelieve in real benefits. A savings account paying 5% interest is often simply assumed to be providing income. If one hears that the inflation rate is 4%, one may still feel that an income is being produced, if one overlooks the taxes required on the fictitious income. Suppose that in this situation one has a 28% tax rate. $100 invested will yield $5 interest on which the tax will be $1.40 for an apparent after-tax income of $3.60. However with 4% inflation, we will have lost $4, resulting in an overall real loss of 40¢ ($3.60 minus $4). If one attempts to spend such savings account "income," exhaustion of principal will be underway.

On the other hand, some mistakenly caution against spending income derived from equities for a similar reason. Yet if the company is reinvesting a portion of its income, as is the customary practice, this is likely to be real rather than merely apparent income and may usually be spent with no impoverishment. Gaining an overall view of benefits and how they are derived helps tailor potential results to one's objectives.

Savings Accounts Are Risk Free

While much better protected against financial risk than many other investment forms, they are not immune. Savings accounts leave the investor totally vulnerable to purchasing power risk, which as we shall see is of major importance across time. The astute investor may want to achieve a comprehensive grasp of the variety of risks with which he may be beset and what risk may lurk behind each investment medium. Without an overall picture of potential risks and benefits, the investor is left to wander without a clear objective across a minefield.

Emotional Hazards

Disturbances That Impair Results

Prompted by strong emotions, one may modify, suspend, or even abandon critical review and judgment. Strong positions may be discarded and absurd ones rashly assumed when moved by pulse-pounding emotions. Signals from the investment world from time to time are apt to stimulate the emotions. If untempered, destructive emotions may not only sow havoc in one's portfolio of investments but also lead directly and independently of financial condition to general discontent.

Ignorance is the ally of the destructive emotional forces, salient among which are impatience, greed, fear, and ego involvement. Knowledge puts them in perspective and undercuts their destructive potential. To be truly helpful, knowledge must be integrated into daily living by practice or insight. Otherwise, knowledge remains compartmentalized and only tentatively available to offset older incompatible beliefs. Such experientially isolated knowledge is often referred to as "intellectual" as opposed to "emotional" insight.

Impatience

The most corrosive aspect of impatience is what psychologists call "inability to delay gratification." It is one of the robust predictors of misery and failure in life. Limited ability to delay gratification is also one of the great causes of needless loss, forgone advantage, and finally of discontent in investing. For the honest nonprofessional, successful investment involves the patient pursuit of a long-term strategy. The only ones to make profits on quick short-term transactions, apart from those who offset them with equally large losses, are few: real experts operating within their special area of expertise, the fabulously lucky, or crooks. Moreover, if one averages in the time spent in study and preparation for experts and crooks, (some of the latter may spend their time in confined repentance rather than preparation) the quick payoff may not really be so quick, and the amount possibly only commensurate with an ordinary salary.

Without patience, a long-term strategy will unravel and may degenerate into the stimulus-controlled moves of the impulsive gambler. For such an externally directed lost soul, a tip, lucky number, or coincidence may inspire a hunch, wish, or desperation move.

With patience, a desired goal may be persistently pursued by an appropriate strategy. This not only increases the likelihood of attainment, but also that what is attained reflects the individual's desires. Patience in pursuit of a goal does not mean that one may not want to reexamine goals or strategies; but it does imply that if reexamination finds them appropriate, then one may persevere with cheerful acceptance even in the presence of temporary adversity.

Greed or Inordinate Acquisitiveness

Among those whom you as an investor will encounter will be some who intend to make money from your actions. They may assail you with advertisements and newsletters or talk to you directly or through your television set. They may pander to and whet your appetite for a windfall of riches.

You do not really need them for this purpose: you can trap yourself quite effectively. You can implant desire by flooding your mind with tempting visions. You can amplify desire to an artificial need by holding on to the tantalizing visions and thinking they should be yours. You can bolster your urgency by telling yourself that you can, must, and will have these things.

Beyond this, you can undermine your critical judgment. You can do this by flooding yourself with unopposed irrational cant tending to prevent critical thinking. If you should begin to reason, you could counter with thoughts about the facts like, "This information is not wholly objective," or "Who really knows?" or "We are entering a new phase now where past landmarks no longer hold." The truth in these thoughts may seem to make them plausible. We can be misled by such thoughts if we ignore the probable degree to which we hold effectively approximate knowledge, accuracy in our data, and historical relevance in market norms.

By tantalizing ourselves and thwarting critical judgment, we can let greed whip us to such a frenzy that we put all our money on Soon Bust Corporation since now we know it will treble in the next month. Furthermore, we can afford to ignore the price, because even if it is up much higher when we buy, only doubling our money still is not so bad. But wait, if we know it is going up, why limit our investment to our own resources? We can borrow money to buy more.

We can do all the above and produce the losses that come from following greed and excluding critical judgment. We can invest according to methods and in commodities or issues about which we have led ourselves to believe that, for no significant risk, a fortune can be made immediately for only a trivial expenditure of money, time, or understanding. But we do not have to do this. We can wield critical judgment and shun greed. We can do this by reversing the steps. We can dispel greed by keeping in mind the idea that while there may be some merit in an accumulation of money and the things it can buy, beyond a minimum point, the returns diminish and soon further additions cease to be significantly relevant to a good life. We can cultivate critical judgment by practice and by recognition of its virtue in helping us reach optimal decisions throughout life in many areas: financial, personal, political, and social.

Fear

The insistence of fear can push one into needless losses. In a crashing market, selling in a panic can devastate our assets. Since the markets frequently overreact to news, positive or negative, if one sells automatically upon bad news, one may very well be taking needless losses. The loss may be needless because the issue may not have undergone any significant long-term damage. The loss may also be needless, even when a sizable setback has occurred, if the issue's price has sunk to an excessively low level. Bad news, whether from misfortune or simply falling prices, dictates action. However, the action is to investigate to see how values have been affected relative to prices. For example, in 1929 when the market crash began, investigation would have shown dangerous overvaluation and indicated that stocks be sold. However, in 1932, the situation was reversed; by then, prices had sunk far more than prospects. At that time, stock purchases would have done very well indeed. Nevertheless, some people scared by the relentless depression feared that everything would be lost; in desperation, they sold off assets at a fraction of their value.

Splendid opportunities may be lost because of fear. The best opportunities often exist in an atmosphere of pessimism. The fearful may hesitate to move into markets or issues about which there is widespread disenchantment, thereby foreclosing bargains. Likewise, particular markets or issues may be shunned due to unrealistic fears.

Where fears are unrealistic, knowledge encourages freedom of action and comfort. Where fears are realistic, knowledge and critical judgment promote appropriate precautions and hence safety and comfort.

Ego Involvement

Some define their worth by their possessions. If their possessions are extensive, expensive, interesting, crude, shocking, the right style, or anything else thought to reflect power, status, astuteness, membership in an esteemed group, etc., then they may hope to bask in the reflection. This is, of course, an egregious mismeasurement of oneself. Using this mismeasure produces misery for the user, even when it might seem to be working. A secondary concern, appropriate to us here, is that it also gets in the way of successful investing.

To that extent you treat your investments as an extension or reflection of yourself you hinder objective critical appraisal. One may not be able to recognize an unfortunate choice for what it is until deterioration has progressed to monumental proportions. You may keep hoping that your incisive choice will be vindicated. Conversely, if you doubt yourself, you may doubt your choices and, seeing something appreciate, sell it prematurely because it seems to lack the underlying strength or value.

To counter this tendency: (1) gain some knowledge of investment value, (2) practice objectively appraising value, (3) accept both your fallibility and your capability for insight, and (4) reject tendencies to value yourself competitively.

Disturbances of Peace of Mind

An investor who generates negative emotions from investing is in danger of eroding happiness. The devastation wrought here overshadows the destructive effects on the monetary results of investments. Besides the direct corrosive effects of impatience, greed, and fear, the following distressing conditions may be observed.

The Roller-Coaster Syndrome

In tandem with a rise in an investment's value, some investors' moods rise. At this stage, the syndrome may seem great. An elevating mood lifts spirits and energy. The afflicted may effuse that life is a glorious feast where one dines on meat and honey, wines flow freely, and laughter, beauty, and love surround. But the observer may also notice restlessness, feelings of invincibility, and on occasion, a recklessly foolish plunge into some new venture.

However, even if the afflicted escapes a rash venture, the market will be true to itself. It will fluctuate. After going up, it will come down, and so will the person afflicted with this syndrome. After the warming fires of elation, the sufferer reaps the cold ashes of desolation.

Not all those afflicted suffer to this degree, but for many, it is unpleasant. For many, the causes are largely a reflection of their ideas. The prototypic sufferer reveals ego involvement. His self-appraisal depends on his investment results. Cutting this link is important. So is more thorough market knowledge. So also is the establishment of a better perspective on wealth and status.

Preoccupation

In brokers' firms, you may see a number of people sitting and watching the ticker reporting current transactions. Others keep continual track of the markets by television, newspaper, and computer. There is no reason to believe that this kind of hovering over one's investments, investment possibilities, or the business environment will be in any way helpful; indeed, as the reader will see, there is some ground to think this can impair results. Be it monetarily helpful or not, it is life-constricting.

Excessive Importance

Managing one's savings can only produce benefits in a few of life's many facets. Slighting other areas is to squander life. Investment management is intended to enhance life. Therefore, the chapter on optimizing benefits will give some attention to contending with problematic emotional forces.

CHOICES

An obvious statement of the investor's purpose may be readily forthcoming: to make money. But if one delves no more deeply into one's purposes than this, one is preparing the ground for confusion and contradictory tactics. One's purposes properly influence the choice of investment media, the selection of specific investment choices within each medium, and the investment tactics to be used. A specific investment may be best suited to one or more of the following goals:

1. Preserving Savings
   a. Nominal Savings
   b. Real Savings

2. Producing Income
   a. Reliably
   b. Maximally
   c. Increasingly

3. Growth of Capital
   a. Reliably
   b. Maximally

It is possible for these three objectives: preservation, income, and growth, to be simultaneously satisfied by one investment. However, the contribution of potential investment alternatives to each of these three objectives will vary. While some investments may provide the prospect of moderate preservation or safety, moderate income, and moderate growth, this may not be just what you want. If you primarily want to preserve your savings, you may be quite unhappy with only moderate safety. Wanting either the greatest income or a giant increase in wealth, one will scorn such moderate prospects.

Although all three purposes may be served by a strong and profitable enterprise, the attempt to maximize one objective may work to the detriment of the others. For example, since growth is fueled by reinvestment of income, the payment of high dividend will diminish the corporate income available for reinvestment and may thereby place constraints on growth. For another example, spectacular growth is often enabled by entry into new fields or employing new methods; but this will normally increase risk and drain cash available for dividends.

Therefore, one may want to give the three possible objectives comparative weights. For instance, if one likes numbers, weights from zero to ten could be assigned to each major objective to indicate respectively minimum to maximum importance. If for the three objectives one assigned a total of fifteen points, one would have a profile of relative importance. Thus, a seventy-five-year-old person who wants income to last him for life might assign weights as follows: safety 5; income 10; growth 0. However, if he were also concerned about passing an inheritance to his grandchildren and had a current income sufficient to his needs, then his weights might be as follows: safety 7; income 3; growth 5.

This kind of comparative consideration would help the investor in his decision about degree of acceptable risk, type of acceptable risk, the preferred type of benefit, and the time span of primary concern. While a safety 4; income 4; and growth 7 profile has the priority on growth, it is clearly different from a safety 2; income 3; and growth 10, which would reflect a much more exaggerated and reckless concern for growth.

I use numerical weights only as an example. I do not mean to say that the investor ought to use such weights; but, if he does, two advantages may be achieved. First, by forcing one to choose between desirable objectives, the investor is led to a comparison of rival goals that otherwise might not be made. Second, for the numerically inclined, the application of such numbered weights when considering specific investment criteria may help to sharpen the suitability of the final choices.

The three major goals—preservation, income, and growth—each embrace alternatives. With regard to preservation, the investor should clarify whether he or she wants to preserve nominal or real wealth. This is one question that simply asking may answer.

You may want to make your income as large as possible. Or you may choose to have reliable yearly income. Thirdly, you may want income growing across time. The latter is likely to appeal to someone contemplating growing obligations as from growing children. Again, you may accent reliably growing or maximally growing income, etc.

If you want maximal capital growth, you may want to soar with the high-fliers. If you want reliable capital growth, you will give greater consideration to sustained patterns even if at more moderate rates.

I urge you to reflect on your own purposes as you read. Given at least a minimum knowledge of investments, if you reflect on your true ends, you will not only discern your objectives. You will also sense the degree of risk to which you are temperamentally suited. You will appreciate the kinds of risks you are willing to take. You will be equipped to make enlightened investment choices appropriate to your situation. Specific investment planning must begin with your values and choices. What is most important to you?

PART TWO

INVESTMENT BACKGROUND

Chapter 4

Investment Vehicles

Let us next look at the things available for investment. Our purpose here is not only to achieve some familiarity with the more important forms of investment but also to know something about their investment qualities. To do this, we have to know something about the major attributes of issues and their impact on risk and benefit. Accordingly, the material is presented under two classifications in order to point up two of the most important aspects of securities: (1) who issued them and (2) their form, principally whether their monetary value is fixed or flexible.

CLASSIFIED BY ISSUER

Corporate Securities

These are pledges or acknowledgments of property rights over the corporation's capital. They exist in four main forms: stocks, bonds, convertible issues, and warrants or rights.[1]

Stock

Stock represents ownership of the company. As owners, stockholders have a residual claim on their company's assets and income. That is, their ownership represents what is left after all of the specific claims of creditors have been satisfied.[2] Stockholders have a number of specific rights depending upon the kind of stock they hold. Periodic payments to the holders of stock are called dividends because they represent a division of profits. Stocks have several forms: common, preferred, or convertible. They may be further defined by the corporate charter into special classes.

Common Stock

The common stock is the most complete or true form of stock ownership. Although infrequent, sometimes special classes of common stock are created by a company's charter, which alter their characteristics. Then common stock may be designated as class A, B, or C. Such classification of common stock is not usual. Normally, common stock has the following characteristics:[3]

Residual Claim on Assets and Income

The common stockholder has the most junior standing in legal claim to a share in assets and income. His or her share is what is left over after all other legitimate claims have been satisfied, including those of the preferred stockholder.

Participates in Growth

Common stockholders benefit directly from a company's growth. Since their claim is residual, as the company's net income and assets grow, they are the legally recognized beneficiaries of the additional value. Though employees and others benefit indirectly, common stock is the only avenue of direct participation in growth.

Voting Power

As the legal owners, stockholders have a voice in the direction of the company's activities expressed by their vote. Normally they vote for the board of directors, for the selection of an auditor, and for special resolutions placed on the ballot. They also have the corollary right of placing propositions on the ballot if they have sufficient support. The stockholder has a vote for each share of stock he possesses. When more than one class of common stock exists, the most frequent alteration is the denial of voting power to one class. Developers sometimes arrange this to prevent control being stripped from them.

Preferred Stock

The name *preferred* refers to the priority in claim to assets and income, which preferred stockholders enjoy over the claims of common stockholders. In the payment of dividends and in the distribution of assets upon liquidation, the preferred stockholders' claims must be completely satisfied before anything goes to common stockholders. Their position is a curious hybrid between creditors and owners, or between owners of bonds and common stock. They are properly regarded as a stock because their claims may simply be put aside if funds are insufficient. Yet they may be thought of as creditors because they do not share in growth or decision making and their dividend like the bondholder's interest is fixed by the terms of the issue. Although called a dividend because its payment is mandatory only if sufficient income exists, from the standpoint of the preferred stockholder, the preferred payment resembles interest more than a dividend because it is less flexible and deprived of the possibility of growth.

Preferred stock may have several provisions.[3] The most important for the investor to be aware of is that, like bonds, preferred stock may be callable. For issues that are callable, the issuing company has the right after a certain date to buy back the stock at a stipulated price, known as the call price. Of course, this right will only be exercised if the market price for the stock is higher than the call price. Preferred stock may or may not be cumulative. If the dividend is not paid because funds are insufficient in a particular year, cumulative stock requires that in subsequent periods when income may become available, the company must pay off all back as well as current dividends owing on the preferred before proceeding to the payment of dividends on the common stock. Preferred stock, like bonds, may also be convertible. *Convertible* means that at the holder's choice, the issue may be changed into common stock. Participating preferred has the right to a further share in any dividends after the payment of the stipulated dividend. The arrangements for participation vary. However, very few issues have this feature.

Bonds

A bond represents evidence of debt. Bondholders are thus creditors of the company. A bond is an obligation to repay the principal sum at a stipulated time, which is called the date of maturity. It usually is also an obligation to pay periodic interest, normally semiannually. The term interest for these periodic payments reflects its status as a reimbursement for the temporary use of money and the bondholder's status as creditor. Bonds, like preferred stock, frequently have a "call" provision whereby the company can, at its initiative, redeem the stock at a specified price after a certain date. Bonds are redeemed either by maturing or by call.[4]

Priority of Claim

Bonds differ in the priority of their claim. A bond with a prior claim represents a safer instrument, since its claim has to be satisfied before the claims of bonds of lesser priority. Although this is an important feature of a bond, it is usually not revealed by the name, which typically, in addition to the interest on the face value, signifies either one or a combination of the following aspects: (a) security, like debenture; (b) purpose, as refunding; or (c) a special feature, like "sinking fund." An advisory service like Moody's or Standard & Poor's is particularly helpful to an investor who wishes to know the essential features and investment merits of an issue.

Security

Bonds vary in the nature of the security or collateral pledged to the repayment of the bond. Some bonds are accompanied by a lien on assets, while others are not. Debentures are not secured by a lien on specific assets. For those bonds that are secured, there is great variation in the nature of the security. First mortgage bonds are secured by a primary lien on specific assets of the company.

However, I caution you that the safety of a bond does not primarily reside in the presence, absence, or priority of liens. The small investor should be more concerned with the general continuing financial strength of the issuing company. An unsecured bond of a financially robust corporation is infinitely better than a first mortgage on the special machinery of a tottering company. First, the resale value may have little relation to the book value of the property, especially if there is no use for it. Second, regardless of the basic value, a great deal of somebody's time and effort will be required to make the disposal arrangements.

Registration

Newly issued bonds are now typically registered to the owner. Registered bonds pay interest and finally principal only to the registered owner. Until recently, most bonds were unregistered and called bearer bonds. They had detachable interest coupons to be surrendered for the payment of interest. Whoever had physical possession of the bond or coupon was deemed the owner, hence the name "bearer."

Convertible Issues

Conventionally and technically, convertible issues are either bonds or preferred stock. However, I have classified them together in a separate heading in order to represent their investment nature. Convertible bonds and convertible preferred stock are hybrids. They may be converted to common stock at the demand of the holder, thereby having a potential claim on ownership and growth. Thus, their performance as investments has dual features. They perform at times and in some respects as common stock. They also perform in some ways as bonds or preferred stock.

The conversion into common stock occurs at the owner's election according to a set ratio, for example, perhaps two common shares for each share of preferred stock. In such a case when issued with, say, a value of $100, the common might be selling for $25. Clearly, if the owner converted at that time, he would lose money, for he would wind up with two times $25 for his $100. This excess reflects the premium paid because the convertibility gives the prospect of growth. If five years later the common is selling for $70, conversion into common would result in a market price of $140. Thus, convertible issue price and existence are influenced by the price and dividends of the common stock. As the price of the common stock approaches parity with the price of the bond or preferred stock times its ratio of convertibility, the convertible issue will move up or down in price together with the common stock. One reason for not converting when parity or even a surplus over parity is achieved is that the convertible usually carries a higher yield. Thus the holder is likely to prefer to continue to receive the higher yield while enjoying the same price appreciation. Of course, if the common dividend grows and the convertible interest or dividend remains fixed, the common dividend might eventually surpass the convertible.

Because the convertible has priority features over the common and initially a higher yield, it has more downside protection than common stock. If the common loses all potential appeal, the convertible will behave as if it were either the bond or preferred stock that it also is. It appears therefore that convertible issues combine the advantages of common with the advantages of the bond or preferred stock. The compensating drawback is that having such an advantage, they customarily sell at a premium. Thus, their price is usually somewhat higher than that of the equivalent common or the equivalent nonconvertible bond or preferred stock.

It has been said that convertible issues should be shunned because they "are neither fish nor fowl." It is true that they are neither simply one or the other. They are rather fish with the power of flight; birds with the ability to swim submerged. They combine the advantages of both. The shortcoming is that they accordingly are more expensive.

Warrants and Rights Issued by the Corporation

Warrants are rights that give the holder an option to buy a certain number, usually a fraction, of shares of common stock at a specific price. Warrants may be attached to an issue of bonds or to an issue of preferred stock. As a management incentive, companies have issued long-term stock purchase option warrants. Typically these warrants enable the holder to buy the stock at prices above the current market value. Thus they have no immediate arithmetic value, but in providing an avenue of possible growth, they have a potential value.[3]

When a corporation wishes to expand its investment capital by issuing new stock, subscription rights may be issued to the common stockholders of a certain date according to the number of shares owned. These rights enable the holder to subscribe to a number of shares of the new issue. The purpose of these subscription rights is to permit stockholders to maintain their proportional ownership of the company upon the advent of a new issue of common stock.

Warrants and rights may be exercised or traded. When simply exercised by the recipient of the issue as intended, they are not especially remarkable for the holder, except as an opportunity to share in the growth or to maintain one's proportionate share. Nor is the sale of warrants received from issue especially remarkable. One is simply taking the value in cash instead of stock. However, the purchase and sale of warrants or rights is a highly leveraged and consequently speculative undertaking. The market value of a warrant springs from the difference between market price of the common stock and the price specified in the warrant entitling the holder to purchase stock. The value is that difference divided by the number of warrants required to purchase one share of stock. A moment's reflection will reveal how volatile the price of warrants is. Let us assume that ten warrants can be exercised to buy one share of stock for $100. If the price of the stock moves from $100 to $101, there is only a minor movement for the stock; but the warrant has gone from worthless (at $100, you do not need the warrant to buy at $100) to 10¢, an infinitely large increase. If the price moved from $100.25 to $102, the stock has moved 1.7% while the warrant has moved from 2.5¢ to 20¢, an increase of 700%.

Like convertible issues, warrants threaten to dilute common stock. That is, as additional common shares are issued without fully equivalent value being injected into the company, the value represented by the common stock erodes.

Limited Partnership Securities

In an effort to avoid double taxation, a number of small-to-medium size companies having small capital needs opted to be formed as partnerships rather than corporations. Indeed, some of these are reformed companies. Their securities being listed on major stock exchanges are readily marketable and except for (a) tax consequences, (b) limitations in liability, and (c) dichotomization of partners into general and limited classes having distinctive powers and obligations, are in other respects analogous to corporate securities. However, since legislation dictated a tax on gross income, many publicly traded partnerships will convert to corporations, so I shall say no more about them.

Government Securities

Government securities consist only of bonds and other evidence of debt. Normally they are unsecured, but some provide that specific revenues of governmental bodies are pledged and some government instrumentalities may mortgage property.[3]

United States Government

U.S. government securities are of the highest quality since there is almost no risk that the government will not pay interest and debt at full dollar value. If nothing else, this assurance comes from the government's influence over the money supply. Historically the U.S. has always paid the principal and interest on its debts.

U.S. debt consists of (1) public issues and (2) special issues. Special issues are sold by the treasury to specific government instrumentalities that have money to invest. They are unavailable to the investor. Public issues are as follows:

Nonmarketable

Nonmarketable issues cannot be traded or transferred. They may be purchased from the government or one of its instrumentalities or agents, and they may be redeemed through similar channels. Of necessity, therefore, these issues have no fluctuating market price. Savings bonds are the issues of interest to the investor here. They may be bought or redeemed at banks, post offices, or through the Treasury Department in Washington, D.C. They are offered in a number of series whose characteristics change as the issuance of one kind supersedes older ones. The characteristics of new issues will be determined by prevailing money market conditions.

Savings bonds are sold with stipulated interest rates, dates of maturity, and dollar denominations. They are issued in denominations that vary in face value from $25 to $1,000. For the most part, interest is realized only in the increasing value of the bond and therefore is taken when the bond is redeemed. Typically their interest rates increase slightly the longer they are held. They may be redeemed at the holder's option after a brief initial period. Although they have stipulated dates of maturity, the bonds may continue to earn interest beyond those dates.

Savings bonds are well protected from all important risks except for inflation to which they are completely unprotected. They are extremely unlikely to be defaulted so there is no appreciable financial risk. Since they are unmarketable, there is no risk from fluctuating market prices. Since they may be redeemed at the owner's option, they are very liquid. Since they are registered to the owner, they have some protection from destruction and theft.

Marketable

These marketable U.S. government securities may be purchased when issued through the Federal Reserve or subsequently over the counter through a broker. Since they are traded, they have a price that will rise or fall with the vicissitudes of the market. This introduces an element of risk not present in the unmarketable issues. The degree of the market risk, as we shall see later, will increase with the time remaining to the issue's maturity.

Several kinds of issues are available. They vary mainly in time and method of receiving interest. In ascending order of length of time to maturity, the issues of interest to the individual investor are as follows:

a) Treasury bills have the shortest term to maturity. They mature typically in ninety or ninety-one days from date of issue. Treasury bills are issued at a discount from face value. The interest is received when the bill is sold and is the difference between the amount paid and the amount received at sale or redemption.

b) <u>Treasury certificates of indebtedness</u> are offered initially at par and pay a fixed rate of interest. They usually mature in about one year.

c) <u>Treasury notes</u> are like the certificates, but are somewhat longer-term instruments, maturing in from one to five years.

d) <u>Treasury bonds</u> are the long-term issues. They are originated with maturities that vary from five to forty years. The investor should be aware that often these bonds have <u>call</u> provisions. That is, after a certain date, the treasury may call or redeem them at a stipulated value. Since the attraction of a long-term issue to an investor is locking into a high rate of interest for a long time, this feature is important because it places this lock in jeopardy.

Municipals

The name *municipals* is applied to securities issued by all nonfederal governments within the United States. This includes all those obligations of the various states, counties, townships, taxation districts, and agencies of state and local governments. They vary widely in characteristics. <u>Perhaps the most important characteristic of a bond is the credit worthiness of the issuer</u>. This varies sharply across issuers and across time. The investor is best guided by the ratings of professional analysts.

Interest received from some municipals is nontaxable by the federal government and also usually by the issuer. Federal nontaxability rests upon constitutional interpretation given by the Supreme Court of the United States early in this country's formative period. Frequently bills are submitted to Congress to reverse this, but this has never happened. However, the 1986 tax reform introduced a change that created some uncertainty. Truly public issues, perhaps like state general obligation bonds, and quasi-public issues, perhaps like those for the funding of hospitals, will remain free of direct tax although quasi-public issues will be included as a preference item under the alternate minimum tax. However, issues deemed to be private in character, such as bonds to finance a stadium, will henceforth be taxed. There is still uncertainty about both the demarcations and validity of the distinctions.

The following distinctions in the backing of a municipal are worthy of note:[5]

General obligation

These bonds are issued by governmental units (a) having unlimited power to raise taxes to pay debts and (b) pledging themselves to pay without limitation. However, there may be political or economic barriers to this. Most state, county, and city bonds are of this type. These are more likely to remain tax-exempt, but the investor should require definite legal opinion on this point before committing funds.

Limited obligation

Tax-Limit Bonds

Some cities, counties, and taxation districts have limitations on their power to levy taxes. Such a limitation will have an uncertain negative implication regarding repayment. It is uncertain because it depends on both the nature of the limitation and the other obligations outstanding, which are subject to change.

Revenue Bonds

These bonds are payable solely from the revenues of a publicly owned property, which provides services for which fees are charged. If the revenues are insufficient to pay, the associated municipality is under no obligation to provide other funds. On the other hand, some projects from which revenues are pledged may provide a more reliable source of funds for payment of interest and principal than the general obligation of the state. In such a case, these may be preferred over a general obligation bond.

Market Contract Creations

There are a number of contractually derived market products that were initially designed to provide hedge mechanisms, but that also may be used by themselves alone, or as "Texas hedges." A hedge is the use of one position to counterbalance the risk of another. A Texas hedge is where both positions augment the same risk.

Options

An option is a market contract that gives the holder the right to buy or sell a certain amount of a particular stock or commodity at a specific price before a specified date. A call is an option to buy. An option to sell is a put. One may buy or sell a call or buy or sell a put. The option writer sells the option to an option holder. The holder has the right to exercise the option, while the writer has the reciprocal obligation to buy or sell, in return for which he receives a premium, which is the price paid for the option.

Futures Contracts

A <u>futures contract</u> is a binding legal agreement to buy or sell something at a certain date in the future at a specified price. That something may be a commodity to be delivered later or a financial abstraction that is incapable of delivery. As the contract expires, the holder can either proceed to its execution or, as is more usual, offset or cover his position by a new transaction. Thus, if one had bought, one could now sell.

Commodity Futures

Commodity futures contracts were originally created as devices to protect primary producers and processors of agricultural commodities. They found that they could protect themselves against adverse price fluctuations by making agreements ahead of time for later delivery. The farmer in summer could sell his fall wheat at today's reasonable price and protect himself should prices fall. The miller, likewise, could buy his fall wheat at the reasonable price prevailing in the summer and protect himself from rising prices. Those who do this are hedging. They are protecting themselves from catastrophe at the price of forgoing a windfall. Since, however, anyone can buy or sell, commodities can be used for speculative plays. A large number of commodities are available for futures contracts, including metal and other resources.

Stock Market Index Futures

Stock index futures are a relatively recent innovation, which function similarly to commodities except of course that there is nothing to deliver apart from a payment; the amount of which is determined by the interim performance of the particular stock index used. The S&P 500 is perhaps the most well-known of the indices for which futures are traded. The Value Line Index is somewhat broader and gives greater weight to smaller companies than does the S&P. The New York Stock Exchange Composite Index also has futures traded.[7]

These index futures are used by large money managers to maximize current income by arbitrage programs between a portfolio of stocks and a representative stock index future. (Arbitrage simply refers to the activity of making a profit from discrepancies between related markets by simultaneous purchase in one and sale in the other. Arbitrageurs thus provide an unintended service in keeping related markets in equilibrium.) When the value of the index future diverges from that of the stocks by a certain percentage, the undervalued one is bought and the other sold. The index future refers to the price or level of the stock index ninety days after its date of issue. At the expiration of the index future, since no commodity exists to be delivered, accounts are settled by cash, and the arbitrageur simply reverses his transactions. At expiration, a superior income can be earned from the sum of (1) the interest on the treasury bills used as collateral for the futures and (2) the adjustment in price of either or both the index future or stocks to equality at the period end, minus (3) the cost of the transactions. If the index properly represents one's stocks, this may be accomplished at almost no risk.

Index futures may also be used by the individual investor to hedge against systematic risk at particularly critical junctures. For example, if one holds a portfolio of stock for the long-term and therefore does not want to disturb them, but is convinced that in the near term stocks will go down, a hedge may be created by keeping the stocks and selling an appropriate index future. (Be aware that you may be right that the market will go down, but err in its timing.) Also, as with other instruments designed to provide a means of hedging, one may simply speculate with them.

Miscellaneous Issuers

Open-Ended Mutual Funds

For the small investor, these are an important avenue for participating in investments of stocks, bonds, money market instruments, and stock market indices. They may be the preferred form of entry into these investments for the small investor. This is because of their usefulness in providing management, diversification, and expertise for the investor. Thus, they warrant the space for separate description, which will be given in more detail under investment institutions.

Savings Institutions

Although many savings institutions offer some of the securities listed above—for example, banks that issue stock—they also offer a distinct investment medium besides marketable securities. These include savings accounts and certificates of deposit, known as CDs. Certificates of deposit may generally be considered either as nonmarketable original issue discount bonds or as time-limited savings accounts. CDs normally pay a higher rate of interest than savings accounts to compensate for the decreased liquidity.

Savings accounts are offered by commercial banks, savings banks, savings and loan associations, credit unions, and finance companies. Savings accounts are <u>not</u> all identical. The risks and benefits vary widely. Some accounts are insured by federal agencies, such as the Federal Deposit Insurance Corporation (FDIC) for banks, and the Federal Savings and Loan Insurance Corporation (FSLIC) for savings and loan institutions. With their help, a few institutions have gone bankrupt recently with no losses to account holders, at least within insured amounts. Other institutions have a nebulous guarantee; for example, when Manoa Finance became insolvent in Honolulu a few years ago, lengthy legal proceedings were set in motion, which finally resulted in some restitution of losses by the State of Hawaii. Still other institutions have no such outside protection.

As with many other investments, the major protection of the account holder lies with the financial soundness of the institution offering the accounts. In a major calamity touching many institutions simultaneously, it is doubtful that the insurance or guarantees would be very great protection. Intensively regulated and audited institutions having reserve requirements and numerous restrictions in the ways funds may be put to use, such as banks and savings and loans may be expected to be safer than finance companies. However, proposed legislation allowing banks to engage in other activities may change this. Moreover, the cases of the once-venerable banks Continental Illinois and Bank of America have shown how interest rate squeeze or unsound loans can rock even the most apparently secure.

By accepting the somewhat greater risk of accounts that are uninsured and offered by a financially weak or poorly positioned institution, an investor may hope to get a greater return. Such institutions generally need to offer higher interest rates to attract depositors. <u>Indeed, an unusually high rate of interest suggests a correspondingly great increase in risk.</u>

Insurance Companies

Insurance companies go beyond offering protection from specific risks and proffer a number of investment vehicles. Some of these are distinctly investment forms. Others, like nonterm life insurance may offer an uncertain mixture of risk protection and investment.

Private Contracts

Personal loans, rentals, agreements of sale, and other private arrangements present many avenues of investment.

Investments Unattached to an Issuer

Some types of investments are not usually associated with a continuing obligation of an issuer. These are not securities or contracts that the investor holds, but rather, the object itself. One may have a direct investment in commodities, for example by owning gold bullion or coins. This, however, is much more cumbersome and costly than owning stock in a gold-mining company. Likewise, one may own land, objects of art, gems, collectibles, and so forth.

CLASSIFIED BY FORM

Investments may be of the following three forms whose distinctions are of primary importance to the individual investor:

Fixed Quantity of Currency Form

Here, there is an obligation to pay a stipulated sum at a stipulated time or times. The following investment media are of this form:

Fixed-time form

Several fixed-dollar forms of investment are also inflexible with regard to time. They cannot be redeemed whenever one wants. One must wait until stipulated times or events have come to pass before withdrawing one's investment. The following are of this type:

1. Certificates of deposit
2. Insurance annuities
3. Negotiated contracts
   a. Personal Loans
   b. Agreements of sale

4. Bank and S&L money market funds

Flexible-time form

The following fixed-dollar forms of investment have no regularly applied contractual or legal impediments to the withdrawal of one's funds. Savings accounts may have thirty-day waiting periods, but in ordinary situations, these are not used. Marketable instruments may be sold, but there may not always be a ready buyer.

1. Savings accounts
2. Brokers' money market funds
3. Marketable bonds, notes and bills
4. Notes redeemable on demand

Flexible Quantity of Currency Form

Here there is direct ownership of something other than a debt. The thing owned may be tangible or intangible, but its value rests on what others may be willing to pay. What people are willing to pay will, of course, fluctuate. This fluctuating price is a prime attribute not only of flexible-dollar forms of investment, but also of those fixed-dollar forms, which are marketable.

This fluctuating market value may or may not rest on a clearly demonstrable fundamental value, such as utility or beauty. For example, land has a clear fundamental value. People require places to live, grow crops, and conduct their affairs. In contrast to this is the situation of a rare postage stamp. While it may have a postage value of $1, it may be selling for a quarter of a million dollars. The additional $249,999 is only a collector's value not based on the service of any need, beauty, or artistic merit. The collector's demand that sustains that market value is totally arbitrary in that it can never be meaningfully related to another value whether utilitarian or artistic. Thus, with no anchor other than fashion, it could abruptly disappear.

Some may object, arguing that this value is based upon rarity. But rarity of supply only indicates where the price would be fixed for a particular demand. Rarity of supply is not demand. Shark bites are also rare, but nevertheless have little collector's value, at least at present. Although, since the demand here rests upon fashion, I suppose it is possible that some day people will pride themselves on their painfully acquired shark bites, much as dueling scars were once so prized.

The following investment media are of the flexible-dollar form:

a. Tangible: land, precious metals, gems, objects of art, antiques, and publicly traded commodities
b. Securities: common stock and limited partnership depository units

With these securities, the underlying value is ownership of an ongoing organization. The organization's value to the investor rests primarily upon its earning power. Secondarily, the organization has asset values represented by land, buildings, equipment, and ownership of rights (patents, franchises, copyrights, contractual rights, etc.).

Mixed

Convertible issues (bonds and preferred stocks) may be either fixed-dollar form or not at the option of the holder. The fluctuations of the convertible issues' market prices will depend upon a mixture of the influences upon each form. In general, the mixed form combines the advantages of each and have a correspondingly higher premium in price.

Chapter 5

Investment Institutions

THE PRIMARY MARKET

Investment Bankers

Investment bankers initiate the public sale of security issues. They usually do this by purchasing directly from the issuer and arranging a subsequent resale to the investing public at a stipulated price. They will usually also sell at a discount to other investment bankers who will then sell at the stipulated offering price. Except for small issues, they handle this by forming purchasing syndicates to share the risk of being unable to complete the sale. If that should happen, they would be forced to hold the issue on their own account until they could be sold later.

Municipal issues are conventionally required to be sold to investment bankers by competitive bidding. As with the private negotiated purchases, syndicates are formed to make a bid.

The Federal Reserve

One of the ancillary functions of the Federal Reserve is to sell new federal issues to the public.

THE SECONDARY SECURITIES MARKETS

The secondary markets exist to provide a mechanism for the resale of securities after their original sale by the investment banks to individual investors.

Organized Security Exchanges

These exchanges are organized by a limited group of members to provide facilities for trading in designated securities according to rules governing their relationship to each other and to their customers. The New York Stock Exchange is the largest and serve as a model for the formation of the others. The regional stock exchanges are becoming less important with the increasing efficiency of communication and are tending to become specialists in small local issues. The Pacific Exchange, however, also provides for the continued sales of many issues of national interest after the New York exchanges are closed for the day.

The New York Stock Exchange trades only in issues that have been admitted to their list of approved securities. To gain approval, certain requirements must be met primarily involving the provision of adequate information about the securities and their issuers for the benefit of investors. For example, the provision of audited annual and quarterly reports to stockholders is required. Membership in the exchange is open to anyone who can (1) purchase an available seat and (2) pass the scrutiny of an admissions committee as to financial responsibility and moral character.

Trading is conducted around an exchange specialist in the stock of each company by brokers placing specific quotes to buy or sell. The specialist monitors these quotes as they fluctuate within or from a market price, which consists of the range between what has been bid and what has been asked. If a customer's order is "at the market," the price will be established within this range by process of offer and acceptance by brokers. A customer's order may instead specify an exact "limit price," in which case it is noted by the specialist and put aside until the market price reaches that price, if it does within the specified time period. The market price fluctuates up or down according to the relative weight of buy and sell orders. The specialist is required not only to monitor this but also to keep an orderly market, which may mean buying or selling on his own account to offset significant imbalances in momentary supply and demand.

Over-the-Counter Market

This is made up of the thousands of dealers around the country operating out of their own offices who buy and sell securities. Through communication links, a dealer acting on behalf of a buyer or seller can find the best price to complete the transaction in surprisingly little time.

The National Association of Securities Dealers was established in 1939 "(1) to provide regulations and regulatory machinery with a view to preventing fraud, promoting square dealing, and assuring reasonable charges to customers; (2) to secure greater uniformity with respect to both practices and quotations; (3) to establish tribunals for the settlement of disputes among dealers and hearing complaints of customers against dealers."[1] Accordingly, over-the-counter quotations are reported daily through NASDAQ.

THE SECURITIES AND EXCHANGE COMMISSION (SEC)

The SEC was created in 1934 in the aftermath of the stock market crash of 1929 to establish and police rules controlling the exchange of securities. Among its several activities, the SEC registers all organized exchanges engaged in interstate commerce. All issuers of securities on those exchanges are also required to be registered. Those registered must conform to rules promulgated by the commission and other pertinent laws.

Providing the public with adequate information about securities and their issuers in order to protect investors is one of the SEC's major purposes. Regulations are in force to control certain stock price manipulations and some transactions by corporate executives in the securities of their companies.

BROKERAGE FIRMS

Transactions are usually made for investors by brokerage firms, which have seats on the major exchanges and also can function as over-the-counter dealers. You buy or sell securities by giving your broker an order, which may be either on a "market" or "limit" basis. "At the market" requests that the order be executed immediately at the best currently available price. A limit order specifies a price that must be observed. On a sell order, the price may be no less; on a buy order, no more than that specified.

Commissions are charged for executing transactions and are calculated by formulas that vary from firm to firm and from time to time. Often, the absolute dollar value of commissions increases with the value of the transaction, although the commission decreases as a percentage of the value of the transaction as the total value rises. Thus, several small orders will cost more than one large one for the same total value transacted. Orders to buy or sell are conventionally placed in round lots. These are even multiples of 100 shares. Odd lots or fractions of round lots are executed separately. Some brokers may charge their customers more for executing odd lots transactions.

Brokerage firms may facilitate your trades by lending you money to purchase ("buying_on margin") or by lending you securities to sell ("short selling"). These activities were brought under regulation by the Securities Exchange Act of 1934. Margin requirements are controlled by the Federal Reserve System to discourage undue speculation. Short selling is allowed only under certain conditions (in a rising market) so that speculative short selling by itself could not create a market plunge.

Full-Service Brokers

Function

Full-service firms will not only execute your orders, but are also prepared to render further service such as advice as to what to buy and sell and when to do it. The account executive or registered representative who does this is backed up by the brokerage firm's research department. This department usually includes security analysts who develop detailed evaluative studies of specific securities. Others may be employed to develop comprehensive economic and market forecasts, which when combined with the studies on specific securities may result in current advisory position papers.

Advisory Effectiveness

Unlike mutual funds and newsletter advisory services whose positions and advice are published and therefore susceptible to investigation, brokerage firm advice is rendered privately to each client. Therefore, unless one obtains their position paper, it is impossible to adequately assess their overall effectiveness. For this reason, the following observations are advanced.

In spite of their sometimes impressive resources, brokerage firms' results have not always been equally impressive. In one of the best general books written for the small investor, The Intelligent Investor, Benjamin Graham, a veteran security analyst, alluding to the financial troubles of brokerage houses in 1969 and 1970, says, "A third explanation of the financial trouble finally emerged out of a mist of concealment, and we suspect that it is the most plausible and significant of the three. It seems that a good part of the capital of certain brokerage houses was held in the form of common stocks owned by the individual partners. Some of these seem to have been highly speculative and carried at inflated values. When the market declined in 1969 the quotations of such securities fell drastically and a substantial part of the capital of the firms vanished with them. In effect the partners were speculating with the capital that was supposed to protect the customers against the ordinary financial hazards of the brokerage business, in order to make a double profit there."[2]

Commenting that "this was inexcusable . . . ,"[2] Graham was concerned with the ethical breach. May we not also, however, glean something about the effectiveness of some brokerage house investments? Remember that they lost enough money to endanger their continued existence while being preferentially privy to their own best advice. If they invested according to their own advice, its ability to prevent catastrophe may be called in question. If they ignored their advice, could that not be taken as expert judgment on its value?

The author's personal observation is that a wide range exists with respect to acumen, knowledge, helpfulness, and ethical impulses. The range extends from superb to grab-your-shirt-and-run. I don't mean to impugn investment professionals, this range of merit applies to all human undertakings. Some are insightful, respectful of their client's desires and situations, and sincerely concerned to protect and advance their clients' interests. Others, although knowledgeable enough to pass a qualifying examination, will not be so helpful.

Potential Conflicts of Interest

The structure of the relationships between the broker and customer presents two separate and clear possibilities for a conflict of interest. First, your broker makes his money by commissions on your transactions. Thus at times, he may face a conflict between (1) his desire for commissions by having you trade and (2) giving you the best advice, which might be to patiently hold what you currently own. In the article "Brokers vs. Customers: What Are Your Legal Rights?" "churning," or excessive trading to generate commissions, is said to be "one of the most frequent complaints against investment brokers . . ."[3] While the authors point out that churning "is an actionable violation of the federal securities law and various state common law principles including negligence and fraud,"[3] they also observe that "the determination of whether churning has occurred is not simple or easy to detect."[3]

Second, the brokerage firm also buys and sells on its own account. This also creates a distinct potential conflict of interest. What do they do with their power to make a market for an issue when they want to get out of a bad position in a stock? If you, a small investor, enter their firm seeking advice on what to buy, might there not be some temptation to advise you to buy that stock that the firm owns that has gone sour? Unfortunately, this is sometimes what happens. Their alternative would be to dump it on the market, thereby lowering their received price.

Discount Brokers

Discount brokers provide no service other than executing transactions and, if you wish, holding your securities, managing your cash, and lending you securities or cash for transactions. Specifically, they do not undertake to advise you about what or when to buy or sell. In keeping with their lower overhead, they charge significantly lower commissions. A full-service broker may charge as much as 100% more than a discount broker. Indeed, the difference is large enough that an ordinary customer walking in off the street for his first transaction at a discount broker may get charged 30% less than would a large institutional investor who, because of his credit and the size of his business, has negotiated special rates with a full-service broker. On one particular comparison that I made for participation in a municipal bond fund, the full-service broker quoted a charge 1,000% greater than the discount broker. However, recently some "discount brokers" have begun to supply advisory services upon demand. It remains to be seen what will happen to their prices.

ADVISORY SERVICES

Publications

Publications offer the investor information that he or she may want abound. These exist in such a wide array of quality and usefulness as to merit further comment. Martin Zweig, one investment advisor who has used the wide panorama of advisory service advice as part of one of his indicators, says of the generality of advisory services, "My calculations show that when the bullish percentage gets too high, the market tends to head for trouble, and when it get [sic] too low, as pessimism rises, it's often the time to buy stocks."[4]

Full Service

A few publications offer this wide array: (1) comprehensive data on a wide number of individual issues, (2) analyses of these issues, and (3) advice relating to (a) the buying, selling, or holding of particular issues, (b) the general economic climate and future market prospects, and (c) portfolio construction. Advice from these sources is much less likely to be influenced by considerations other than accuracy and excellence. Since they do not act as your agent in transactions and since their advice is part of the published record on which they may be judged for both patronage and liability, the potential for conflict of interest is minimal.

Standard & Poor's the <u>Outlook</u> and ancillary services and the <u>Value Line Investment Survey</u> are two excellent full-line services. The data contained in the Value Line service is fairly extensive and spans the past sixteen years on each of 1,700 stocks. Each issue is routinely updated every three months, while important new developments within the three-month period are spotlighted separately. In addition, the Value Line format, using both tabular and graphical presentation, facilitates efficient use of the data. Investors can use Value Line's data to form their own conclusions.

Partial or Specialized Service

Information

Some reference works like <u>Moody's</u> are a gold mine of specific financial data and ratings on certain issues. Newspapers like the <u>Wall Street Journal</u> or <u>Barron's</u> present some current information. However, it is probably a mistake to rely on them except in an incidental way for information. First, this would probably induce an unfortunate short-term point of view. Second, by the time the average person reads something in the paper, the market is likely to have already reacted. Third, holding to a general plan until purposely revised is essential for good investing. Too great a concern with daily events may tend to erode the overriding plan.

Technical Analysis

Technical analysis refers to identification of the current market trend and the corresponding near term market prospects by use of general market features. Technical analysis proper, which uses only direct market patterns as predictors, such as the Dow theorists, must be held suspect on the following grounds: (1) studies of market price and volume movements by a number of mathematicians have led to the random walk hypothesis, which holds that in the short run (within periods of several months), these movements are random and can generate no prediction better than a guess as to future movements;[5] (2) technical analysts identify the trends differently from one another; (3) a comprehensive retrospective study of 540 NYSE stocks over a five-year period failed to find evidence that thirty-two conventional technical configurations predicted later price movements;[6] and (4) casual recollection of past technical predictions contains a number of startling and dramatic errors, such as the once highly touted "guru" Joseph Granville, proclaiming a sell signal just prior to the onset of the 1982 bull market and continuing throughout the following year of surging escalation.

There is another body of what I choose to call technical analysis that differs from what is addressed above, because it attempts to identify the current trend and future price movement by using statistical data outside of the market itself. I call it technical because it uses indicators to predict near term direction of market price movements without addressing fundamental data (data relating to earnings and costs) unless they become so extreme as to constitute an indicator. One interesting advisory of this type has been the Zweig Forecast, which uses indices of (1) monetary conditions and (2) investor sentiment as market predictors.[7] As one might assume, the greater the easy availability of money, the more "bullish" is the outlook. That is, the greater the likelihood of a rise in prices.

However, the other index operates contrary to general expectation; popular sentiment is inverted. This flows from the historical finding that popular opinion has been generally wrong about market movements. The more widespread the popular opinion, the greater the error. At market bottoms, when an advance is in store, the public is fearful and pessimistic; at market tops, just before the fall, enthusiasm reigns. Thus, the more pessimism prevails, the more favorable is the indication; the more optimism prevails, the greater is the cause to worry. According to Zweig,[7] this inverse relationship is especially true of the naive investor, but in general also tends to hold for experts (except for insiders), as the record of mutual funds and investment advisory service attests. It applies not only to the stock market as a whole, but also to particular stocks. From my own perspective, it also appears to be true for other areas of investment; for example, gold and land. This is a fundamental and pervasive relationship of which the prudent investor is aware, especially in the extremes.

Stock Market Indices

Various services attempt to portray the overall action of the market or a major segment of the market by publishing indices. The following indices have wide following:

Dow Jones Indices

The most widely known is the Dow Jones Industrial Average (DJIA). This is the most widely quoted index due to history and inertia rather than for representative merit. It measures price fluctuations of thirty very large companies operating in all areas except for transportation and utilities, which have their own Dow Jones indices. Devised before the advent of our modern ease with large calculations, it attempted to portray the action of all industrial stocks, and when taken together with its sister indices of transportation and utilities to provide a composite picture of the whole stock market. It is generally unrepresentative, however, and because of this is best regarded as an index of the market action of the gigantic, mature, and relatively financially stable companies, often called blue chips.

Standard & Poor's 500 (S&P 500)

A much more representative index, it is still biased toward the larger and stabler companies. Because of the mix of its longevity and representatives, it is one of the better indices for studying historical relationships.

Value Line Composite

The Value Line Composite Average is a broad index of the approximately 1,700 stocks covered by Value Line, which are sold on various exchanges and over the counter. It is designed to be much more representative of the typical stock in the market. It is computed as an equally weighted geometric average of the constituent stocks.[8]

The Value Line Industrial Composite will be referred to later as a source from which I have extracted some market norms. It is to be distinguished from the Value Line Composite Average described above. Included in the industrial composite are nine hundred of the larger industrial, retail, and transportation companies other than railroads. This composite index is weighted according to size (total market value) and therefore is a better measure of average portfolio performance.[8]

NASDAQ OTC Composite

This is a measure of over-the-counter stocks. Although many banks and insurance companies are included, these stocks tend to be of smaller, less mature, and more speculative companies. Because of this and its contrast to the more conservative character of the issues on the Dow Jones, a comparison of the actions of the two indices may reveal something of the character of the general market sentiment. In the later more speculative phase of a bull market, the NASDAQ is likely to outperform the Dow Jones.

INVESTMENT COMPANIES

In all investment companies, regardless of the type, the management of a fund invests in a portfolio of securities. The individual investor participating in the investment fund has a proportionate share of the net assets. One investment amounts to a whole portfolio of investments. Investment companies offer three things to the small investor: diversification, expertise, and partial discharge of the chore of management.

Diversification

This important tactic of risk reduction is provided to the investor in a mutual fund. For small investors, adequate diversification by direct ownership may be somewhat more costly. This is because brokerage firms charge proportionately more for small transactions than for large ones. However, if one deals with a discount broker, the added cost of providing diversification in one's own portfolio is not preclusive, except for extremely small portfolios having less than about $4,000.

Handling the Management Chore

The funds do relieve the investor of handling much of the management chore. They spend time and attention on the tasks of selection and timing of transactions. They provide records of everything so that little may be left to the individual investor besides reviewing their performance. However, this comes at a cost. Management fees, accounting and legal fees, clerical services, rent, office expenses, and so forth are incurred and constitute the accretion of a whole business in itself. The result is an overhead expense, which acts as a continual drain on the profitability of the underlying portfolio of investments.

Expertise

The managers of mutual funds are schooled and experienced in investing. They utilize the advice of equally experienced people who, generally, must be regarded as intelligent. Yet, for all their qualifications, these experts have not done an impressive job. Taken as a group and over a long period of time, mutual funds have failed to justify the added costs incurred, unless you assume that otherwise the individual investor on his own would have stupidly squandered his savings.

They have failed to exceed the performance of the Standard & Poor's 500, which would be the chance expectancy of simply purchasing diversified, nonspeculative stocks and holding them. In 1973, Graham, looking at the results of the ten largest mutual funds, observed that "the overall results for these ten funds for 1961-1970 were not appreciably different from those of the Standard & Poor's 500."[9]

For the period from 1982 through 1986, I calculate, from the data presented by The Individual Investor's Guide to No-Load Mutual Funds,[10] that on the basis of total return, the S&P 500 increased a total of 246%. During that same time period, the guide reports that the highest performance of any no-load mutual fund was 206% while the median return of the top 50 funds was 159.6%.[10]

Zweig, commenting on mutual funds, says, " . . . Numerous studies at the Wharton School of Finance have clearly demonstrated that mutual funds have not been able to beat the returns one could generate by selecting stocks randomly . . . or even by literally throwing darts at the stock page! . . . In addition, there has been a persistent pattern over the years in which mutual funds hold their greatest relative amounts of cash at market bottoms—the point at which they should be fully invested. Furthermore, they also hold their lowest relative cash balances at market tops—just when they should be highly liquid."[7]

Organizational Arrangement

Open-End Companies—Mutual Funds

An open-end investment company, also called a mutual fund, solicits money from investors, which is then added to its portfolio. When the investor wants to redeem his investment, his share of the equity capital is liquidated. Since its equity capital expands or contracts as investors want to buy or sell, the name *open end* is applied.

Load Funds

Traditionally, the investor putting money into a mutual fund was charged a sales commission. This commission, or "load," went to whoever sold the fund shares to the individual. Funds charging sales commissions are called load funds. A typical charge is about 8.5% of the total amount paid. This is a hefty charge and significantly diminishes the capital left to work for the investor. This amount can only be recouped if the particular fund outperforms the alternative, which otherwise would have been selected. Had the capital not been expended at the outset, it would have itself been compounding. Recently, a few funds emerged charging a significantly smaller commission. These are called low-load funds.

No-Load Funds

As their name implies, they make no charges for entry into the fund. Interestingly, their performance is no worse than that for load funds. Indeed, according to The Individual Investor's Guide to No-Load Mutual Funds, "Funds with loads, on average consistently underperform no-load funds when the load is taken into consideration in performance calculations."[11]

Closed-End Companies

The closed-end investment trust is organized as a regular corporation whose business is to invest in a portfolio of securities. You participate in the "fund" by buying its shares, which are sold on regular stock exchanges. They are called closed-end because, like any other ordinary corporation, only so much stock at any time is authorized to be issued. As mutual funds have become more popular, closed-end companies now account for only about 5% of all investment trusts.

Investment Policy

Funds have various policies of investment. Balanced funds are generally tailored to include holdings in stocks, bonds, convertible issues, and cash equivalent funds. They usually attempt to provide adequate safety, moderate growth, and good income. Special-purpose funds exist to emphasize a particular objective after which they are usually named. There are, for example, aggressive growth funds, tax-exempt funds, income funds, growth funds, etc. Some funds specialize in a particular investment medium such as precious metals, utility stocks, international securities, bonds, and stocks.

PART THREE

SCYLLA AND CHARYBDIS

Chapter 6

Risk

All investment entails risk. There is no "sure thing" to protect you from the risk of losing your savings. Investment experts Dowrie and Fuller put it this way: "Not only is risk inevitable, but also it appears in the widest and most unpredictable diversity of forms: scientific advances, wars, catastrophes of nature, fraud, monetary debasement, and an endless variety of political, legal, and economic changes. Where it will strike the investor, he cannot know. Prepare for it he must."[1]

First, attune yourself to where the risks lurk and their approximate dangers. Knowing the sources of risk and their importance, you can then take precautions to limit their damage. To invest profitably, it is important to be familiar with each type of risk so as to be poised to protect against each in relation to its importance.

The pattern of risks and benefits is reminiscent of Scylla and Charybdis, the opposing dangers between and past that Odysseus chose to sail after escaping the deadly beautiful Sirens in order to reach his eventual destination, Ithaca.[2] As with Scylla and Charybdis, to reach the objective, the risks must be approached. Moreover, the risks may lie in opposite directions. Fleeing one may cause running into the other. Yet the investor has more than two opposing dangers, and casual avoidance of one risk may mean flirting with another. Knowing about the dangerous shoals can be helpful in navigating through the investment waters.

Odysseus found that risk was inevitable and would be accepted. In life and investing, to shun all risk will not truly avoid risk. Risks must be accepted so that the greater risk may be discerned and avoided. Accordingly, in order to protect his crew from total obliteration in the whirlpool, Odysseus chose to sail so close to the monster Scylla that its six heads each devoured one of his men.

Were it not for the hope of sailing home, he would not have courted the twin risks. Risk is normally viewed just from its negative side, the risk of loss. It is worth noting, however, that greater risk of loss is overwhelmingly associated with a possibility of increased gain. Risks are undertaken for the benefits, which are believed to be associated with them. A full consideration of risks therefore must also await an understanding of related benefits. However, although some financial risks represent potential for gain, many risks have little or no potential benefit. Managing risk is, therefore, not only a matter of controlling risk, but is also involved with deciding the degree and kind of risk one is willing to tolerate.

SYSTEMATIC MARKET RISK

As the incoming tide raises all that floats and the outgoing tide lowers them, so the market for stocks, responding to various influences, rises or falls, lifting up or casting down individual prices. Because these tides have widespread impact throughout the market, they are called "systematic." Such tides also hit the market for bonds. These systematic influences are especially visible in the most highly organized markets, those for stocks, bonds, and commodities. But in fact, they also buffet the markets for other investment media such as land and collectibles. These systematic influences are the broad market forces acting indiscriminately throughout the market. Although some issues will move contrary to the broad general movement, rising in a falling market or vice versa, even they are affected, for otherwise the price movement might have been greater.

Swings in these systematic market forces create risk. However, as do tides, they tend to fluctuate above and below central or normative levels. Therefore, extreme movements also provide opportunities. (However, caution is in order here because given a long-enough time, norms can change, even for tides.) The major forms of systematic fluctuations are as follows:

Interest Rate Risk

Interest rate fluctuation directly hits the bond market. However, other markets such as stocks and land are also touched. Interest rates rise and fall in response to the supply of money relative to the demand.[3] This is influenced notably by the actions of the Federal Reserve Board in their attempts to influence the availability of money by governmental fiscal policy and by the vibrancy of the economy.[4]

Changes in interest rates <u>necessarily</u> change the price of bonds in an inverse direction. As interest rates rise, the price of bonds falls. This is not a vague tendency, but is a necessary mathematical result. The interest rate on a bond is its yield to maturity. This has two components: (1) the current yield, which is the coupon (or annual payment) rate divided by the price of the bonds; (2) the amortization of the bond's discount or premium across the remaining life of the bond.

For example, let us say we have a $1,000 par bond with one year remaining before maturity and having a coupon or annual payment of 2%, which is selling for 98% of par or $980. The annual payment at 2% of par is $20. The current yield is $20 ÷ $980, or 2% divided by 98%, which is 2.04%. However, if we kept the bond one year for redemption at par value at maturity, there is in addition to the $20 interest, a gain of $20 to be made since the bond for which we paid $980 is redeemed at $1,000. Thus, the yield to maturity is ($20 + $20) ÷ $980 or 4.08%. If, therefore, the prevailing interest rate for a one-year bond of this quality were 4.08%, we might have paid the $980.

Suppose now that the prevailing interest rate rises to 8%. With a coupon fixed at $20, the discount from par must be increased to lift the total yield to maturity to 8%. Therefore, the price of the bond must fall to $944.44. At that price, the $20 coupon plus the $55.56 discount would give a purchaser a total benefit of $75.56 on an investment of $944.44, which is 8%.

The above example not only illustrates that the price of the bond will fall as interest rates rise, but also indirectly reveals that the longer the period to maturity of the bond, the greater will be the rise or fall in price resulting from a change in interest rates. Since the coupon is fixed, the only changeable benefit is the discount or premium. This amount must be amortized over the whole life of the bond. Thus, in a one-year bond, the entire discount applies to that year, but if the life is ten years, that discount must also apply to every year. Hence, the absolute amount of the discount or premium is greater with longer maturities. Thus, the longer the maturity, the greater is the interest rate risk.

To illustrate, on a one-year bond with a 2% coupon bought at par, should the interest rate rise from 2% to 4%, the price would fall to 98.08% of par for a loss of 1.92%. However, for an otherwise identical thirty-year bond, the drop in price would be to 77.2% of par for a decrease of 22.8%. To recapitulate, for bonds having all the same characteristics except for maturity, a rise in interest rates from 2% to 4% would mean a loss of 1.92% for the one-year bond and a loss of 22.8% for the thirty-year bond.

Fluctuations in bond prices from interest rate changes can be substantial. In 1954, long-term treasuries yielded 2.5%. In 1981, they reached 15%.[5] If a change of this magnitude occurred in a moderate period of time (three to five years) on an issue maturing in thirty years, the loss could amount to as much as 80% of the amount invested. In the span from 1982 to July 1986, the yields on such issues dropped to 7.2%,[6] which is a drop of 52%, and correspondingly bond prices on issues having initially thirty years to maturity would have risen over 70%. Swings of these magnitudes are not inconsequential.

The impact of interest rate fluctuations is not confined to the bond market. The value of preferred stock is likewise determined by its yield and responds similarly to interest rate fluctuations, except that having no time of maturity, it responds as an amorphous long-term instrument. Similarly, those common stocks that are valued primarily for their yield, with little consideration given to growth prospects or to ability to circumvent inflation, will tend to respond sharply to interest rate levels. At the present time, utilities are an example. To the extent a stock is viewed in this manner, it will compete with bonds with respect to yields.

There is also a more general, attenuated, and indeterminate sense in which common stocks in general respond to interest rate fluctuations. A decrease in interest rates tends to accompany an expansion in the money supply. As the quantity of money expands, stock prices will tend to rise for two reasons. First, the expansion of money is a boost to the economic activity and hence possible profits of the companies for which the stocks represent ownership. Second, the greater availability of money allows more money to be spent on the purchase of stocks. However, these two reasons only operate fully when the expansion of money eases and alleviates a prior "tightness" (limitation in supply relative to demand) in money that had been restricting economic activity. Moreover, the effect is likely to be obscured by the operation of other factors affecting stocks.

Economic Risk (partially systematic)

The economy swings between depression and boom, recession and recovery. As the general economy fluctuates, business profits react. Here the effect is primarily on common stock, since ultimately the value of stock rests upon the underlying corporate earnings. The magnitude of this risk to stock values is greater than that of interest rate fluctuations on bonds. The widespread suffering of the Great Depression was a result of the Federal Reserve's policy of tight money and the ensuing business retrenchments and failures. These also brought on a severe fall in stock prices.

Although the most obviously disrupted, common stock was not the only investment medium affected. Preferred stock, bonds, lands, and commodities were all touched. <u>Corporate profits may belong to the stockholders, but they are also the primary protection of employees, creditors, customers, and bondholders</u>. Corporate earnings are the primary protection of corporate bondholders even in the case of secured bonds, for often in a time of economic collapse, the security has no marketable value, especially if it is adopted only to the functioning of the defunct organization.

Though other investment media are also affected, common stock carries the brunt of this risk. Bonds, preferred stock, and common stock stand in this order of priority in claim to both corporate assets and income. Before anything can be paid to stockholders, the rights of bondholders must be satisfied in full. Likewise, before common stockholders can receive anything, the rights of preferred stockholders must be completely satisfied.

Finally, it must be observed that only a portion of economic risk is systematic risk. Two factors influence the risk in an unsystematic direction. <u>First</u>, a recession or depression is never absolutely uniform in its impact on businesses. Some industries will be hit harder than others. Thus, there are likely to be industry-specific components to a recession. For instance, in the 1981-82 recession, the construction industry was particularly hard-hit in the aftermath of prohibitive interest rates. In the 1973-74 recession, with OPEC's emergence as a controlling force over energy, utilities dependent on oil were especially hurt. Even in the Great Depression, while financial institutions collapsed, the telephone industry maintained payments to employees, creditors, and stockholders. In general, it may be said that the capital goods industry (those companies that produce the plant and equipment for other companies) will be the hardest hit in a depression. Close to them are the manufacturers of primary construction supplies, such as the steel-producing companies. Least affected are the manufacturers of inelastic consumer products (those having a muted response to price changes), like tobacco or staple food.

The <u>second</u> factor that dilutes the systematic effect of the economic risk has to do with the financial strength of the company and the wisdom or fortune with which it is positioned. Some companies recklessly overextend their resources and become vulnerable to even slight adverse economic circumstances. The same circumstances may have only slight and temporary effects on others in the same industry. In the mid-1980s, many American farmers were failing in their struggle to cope with a disadvantageous change in their market, while others serving the same market were farming profitably. Those in difficulty were apparently farmers who chose or allowed their financial strength to be impaired. Typically out of a desire for rapid expansion or improvement, they borrowed heavily to purchase additional land and modern equipment. The resulting illiquidity and burden of interest payments left them open to devastation when crop prices dropped.

Psychological Climate

Market behavior is ultimately a psychological manifestation. In buying or selling stocks, bonds, land, or commodities, people act as they do elsewhere in life. Notably, forces of conformity, greed, panic, and fashion operate to influence decisions to buy or sell.

However, this does not mean that market behavior is utterly whimsical. Recall that I reject extreme models of humans as either "perfectly rational" or as "irrational." Even a casual glance at the behavior of humans and other animals reveals the capacity to sustain a goal-seeking behavior in a persistent and reasoning manner. Even rats in a maze show this rationality. What encourages some to call humankind irrational lies mostly in the multiplicity, complexity, and disguise of the goals being pursued together with the range and novelty of the methods employed to reach those goals. Thus, if we assume John Doe to be trying to do one thing when he really is much more interested in achieving something else, he may well seem irrational to us.

Therefore, since one of the primary and most widespread reasons for making an investment is to profit therefrom, we are on reasonably safe ground to assume that in the long run, collective investment behavior as reflected in the markets will follow financial facts. From this we can develop approximate norms for fundamental financial value, which ought to hold true for a given culture. Especially in a dynamic culture, our norms may err somewhat; but, when regarded as approximate and susceptible to error and change, such concepts of normative value can be extremely helpful.

Around the normative values, the prevailing psychological climate of fear, appetite, or fashion can create favorites and myths and blow up a gale of over—or undervaluation. For a stretch of a few years, stocks are the quick road to riches. In a twinkling they can become grim specters to be shunned. Particular industries can be "glamorous" or pariahs, specific stocks, stars or dogs. Myths are propounded by gurus and often unquestioningly believed whether accompanied by evidence or not. However, the reality of financial circumstances joined to the goal of profiting from one's investments eventually dispels the prevailing psychological winds, frequently replacing them with their opposites. Thus, winds of varying duration will lift or depress market values; but in the long run, these fluctuations will take place around the normative value.

To the extent that the climate affects an entire market, such as the stock market, the risk is systematic. To the extent that only specific industries or companies are affected, the risk is unsystematic. Systematic market risk is the risk that arises from the fluctuations of the entire market, whether influenced by interest rates, other economic factors, or investor psychology.

These three causes of systematic risk—interest rates, the economy, and investor psychology—all interact. The hurricane of psychological fashion may be generated from a torrid sea of economic and interest rate changes. If the action of one opposes another, the market result will be blunted. More often one is a catalyst to the others creating huge overreactions.

From 1929 to 1932, the Standard & Poor's index plunged from 31.92 to 4.40 for a drop of 86%. Similarly, the Dow Jones dropped from 381 to 41.2 for a loss of 89%. Although less dramatically, systematic forces are still at work. On December 13, 1968, the average price-earnings ratio computed by Value Line for all stocks with earnings was 19.0. On December 23, 1974, this was 4.8, reflecting an erosion in valuation of 75% in six years. More recently and in the other direction, from August 1982 to July 1998 the Dow Jones Industrials rose from 850 to 9,200, a rise of 1,076%.

NONSYSTEMATIC MARKET RISK

Nonsystematic market risk is the risk of loss that attaches to those market fluctuations caused by reasons other than the systematic ones that shape the market as a whole. The source of loss or gain is from within the enterprise itself or its narrow context. Although the source is more narrow, the importance of nonsystematic market risk is as great as, if not greater than, systematic risk. Systematic risk generally reflects fluctuations around a normative value, whereas nonsystematic risk largely represents erosion or enhancement of that basic value.

Financial Risk

Financial risk is what most people think of as risk. It is implicit in the question "Is this a good stock?" This is the risk that the enterprise will decline or flourish financially. The investor is at peril from deterioration in the market price of the issue resulting from the public awareness of weakness, shrinking dividends, or threat of insolvency with terminal distribution of assets insufficient to restore invested principal.

The most likely cause of the above is a deterioration of earning power. This can come from a variety of sources such as competitor's superiority, aging of patents, shifts in market demand, or inefficient operation. It is also possible that while operations remain fundamentally sound and generate increasing earnings, the company's financial weaknesses undermine it. Inadequate liquidity, insupportably heavy debt, or excessive cash demands to support replacement or expansion can jeopardize an otherwise sound venture.

The common stockholder is most vulnerable to this risk. Next comes the preferred stockholder. The holders of unsecured debt such as debentures must be completely satisfied before any payments to any class of stockholder can be made. Secured bondholders may or may not be in better position, depending on the ready marketability of the particular underlying security.

The stellar feature of United States government bills, notes, and bonds is their almost-complete freedom from financial risk. This arises for Americans because of the government's probable determination to faithfully observe its obligations together with its close influence over the money supply. Thus, the problem would probably never be the lack of payment, but would more likely be the impaired value of the money with which payment might be made.

Municipal obligations carry no such freedom from financial risk. In the history of our country, several states have defaulted on their bonds. Each issue must be examined on its own merits. Investors can use published ratings to assess the financial risk of both bonds and stock. The ratings of bonds by Moody's and by Standard & Poor's are published periodically and categorize issues in from nine to eleven classes in order of financial risk. Moody's bond rating of Aaa is the best quality in terms of protection given to the payment of interest and repayment of principal. These judgments rest on several factors, including the adequacy of the coverage of required payments afforded by available funds. Financial risk ratings for common stock are also published by Standard & Poor's, Value Line, and others.

A normal relationship found primarily for bonds, but to a lesser extent and more indeterminate manner for stocks, is for the yield to vary directly with the degree of rated financial risk. Moody's Aaa bonds, being of the highest quality, yield less than other bonds with the same maturity.

Public Favor

This is the unsystematic aspect of psychological risk. The selection by the public of favored and disfavored stocks and industries generates an inverse risk. That is, the more highly a company is preferred, the greater will be the attendant market risk; the greater the disfavor in which it is held, the less the market risk.

This relationship may be viewed from various perspectives. First, the greater the esteem in which an issue is held by experts and public alike, the less room there is for an increase in esteem and the greater the possible fall in adversity. This is even truer when the esteem is not merely expressed as a vague infinitely expandable poetic statement, but rather is expressed in a limited context, such as in the purchase or sale by a limited number of people with limited funds of a fixed supply of items (shares, bars of gold, etc.). In the most extreme case, where everyone wants a particular stock, it will be sold to those who can afford it at the highest bearable price. Note that at this point of extreme favor, there is no further possible upward support available to the issue.

If 100% of all market advisors support a stock, where is the room for increase? There is only one direction for the consensus of advisors to go. In the real world, where nothing is relentlessly advancing with ever-increasing degrees of improvement, a stumble or falter is inevitable. A very minor falter, as an earnings increase of 20% when more was expected, can only begin a downward slide of esteem and market price.

Alternatively, one may measure favor by the price/earnings ratio (P/E) the stock commands. This ratio is simply the market price of the stock divided by the earnings. The higher the multiple, the greater is the esteem with which the market treats the stock. An extremely high P/E ratio represents a vulnerability. On the one hand, a downward readjustment of the ratio becomes increasingly likely as the extremity of the ratio grows. This is a major avenue of price collapse. On the other hand, the higher the P/E ratio, the less the possibility for continued increases in the ratio. Since strong market price rises come from increasing earnings multiplied by increasing ratios, high P/E ratios suggest a diminished likelihood of gain.

Assume this extreme example: last year Buffoons Incorporated did badly and Golden Glitter Company did exceedingly well. Doing so terribly, Buffoons was out of favor and has a P/E of 1. Golden Glitter, however, was awesome and so garnered a P/E of 100. Now, what if this year, each earns just exactly what it did last year, which was appalling for Buffoons and superb for Golden Glitter. Since this year Buffoons earned its whole price in one year (since its P/E was forced down to 1) some people are likely to think it's a bargain, first for being so cheap, and second for halting its earnings slide, which is an achievement. They will buy it, forcing its price upward. Since Golden Glitter failed to improve, it can no longer be seen to justify a P/E of 100 and may well be sold off, forcing its price down.

Viewed from the most basic position, a transition from favor to disfavor will bring a drop in price. This will be amplified to the extent the issue was favored. A transition from disfavor to favor will bring an increase in price. This will be amplified to the extent the issue was in disfavor.

Poor Marketability

A minor risk comes from defects in marketability. If you wish to sell one hundred shares of IBM, you will find the market so strong that it digests the sale, leaving no ripple. In contrast, some issues have so few people interested in buying them that when one wants to sell, one may be able to sell only at a discount. This is likely to be true of very small companies, especially if they are also new. Some companies may even have restrictive covenants regarding sales.

DIRECT FINANCIAL RISK

If you have a savings account in a financially tottering institution, it could be reduced to a memory. If you let a brokerage firm act as custodian for your securities, its failure (if others simultaneously fail and overtax the available insurance) could be a problem; your securities are registered in its name, not yours, and may have been lent to speculators who are now bankrupt. If you own a stock or bond that is unmarketable and it forgoes dividend and interest payments, you take a direct loss. These are all direct financial risks, unsystematic risks which hit you directly rather than through market fluctuations.

PURCHASING POWER RISK

Inflation is a major risk about which many myths abound. Its magnitude is not fully appreciated and derives primarily from being continually cumulative. Since it fairly persistently builds upon itself, its growth across time can be expressed exponentially. For instance, with an inflation of no more than 6.7%, one will have lost more than half the value of a fixed sum of cash in 10 years. Yet in the mid-1980s, people said this was a reasonable, modest, and contained inflation. The remarkably modest level of 2.7%, which some call negligible, would devour one-third of a fixed value in 15 years.

The almost continually cumulative character of inflation is suggested by several observations. Over the past half century, 48 years have been inflationary, 2 have been deflationary, and none have been constant. Thus, inflation has persisted for 96% of the years over the past half century. If we were to set the beginning of 1934 the base for the consumer price index (CPI) at 100, then the 1998 CPI would stand at 1,233.06 with the dollar reduced to 8¢ for a loss of 92% of one's original value across those 64 years. In 2010, it reached 1,617.07. Looked at somewhat differently, if one had placed $10,000 in a bank account in 1934 and treated the interest as income to be spent, by 1951, one would have lost over half of one's value. From 1951 to 1975, one would again have lost half. From 1975 to 1998, one again would have lost 68% of the 1975 value. In 2010, it has lost 32% of its 1998 value.

The large losses indicated above come from our recent history of modest inflation. That losses can become horrendous is shown by experiences in other times and in our own time in other countries. In Germany from 1920 to 1923, prices increased "a trillion-fold,"[7] wiping out even such great accumulations of wealth as university endowments. At such a rate, a billion dollars held three years would be unable to buy a cup of coffee. At that time, Edgar Smith observed, " . . . The demoralization of currency values has completely wiped out the creditor class. The holders of bonds who depended entirely or in large part upon the interest that they received, became paupers."[8]

In 1980, the inflation rate in Israel was 100%. In 1983, inflation in Brazil reached about 130%, while in Argentina it climbed to 300%, then later soaring to the annualized rate of 1,000%.

Inflation is caused by an increase in total dollar spending relative to the flow of goods offered for sale. "If the total flow of purchasing power coming on the market is not matched by a sufficient flow of goods, prices will tend to rise."[7] Important among the various reasons for increases in spending are governmental decisions to spend more than tax receipts, that is, to engage in deficit spending.

If we look to the future with this in mind, we see two things. First, our present rate of deficit spending is staggering. Unless balanced by other equally strong forces, such as the Federal Reserve damping the money supply, inflation looms somewhere beyond the horizon. Second, with a society organized around special interest groups, each of which stands to gain from some particular governmental expenditure, and congressmen whose political life is dependent upon satisfying the most important groups in their area, the budgetary cards are stacked in favor of continuing spending. Do we not, therefore, have a contemporary system that will tilt toward a general continuation of an inflationary tendency, just as we have seen over the past half century?

Before leaving this section on the risk of inflation, let us imagine that we have $100,000 and, not trusting investments, lock our savings in a secret and secure vault where we leave it for ten years. If inflation were kept to what people have called a moderate figure of 6.7% when we returned to get our money, we would find that although it's all seemingly still there, it would only buy half as much as when we put it away. Contrary to appearances, we really would have lost more than half; we would have lost over $50,000 of wealth.

INVESTOR ACTIONS THAT EXPAND MARKET RISK

Fixed Time and Increased Risk

Both systematic and unsystematic market risk can be enormously and unproductively increased by tying one's investment to a fixed time period. The market fluctuates. It moves up and it moves down. The market's movements are often overreactions to current news and guesses. The exact pacing of the ups and downs is known only to the omniscient, of which there are none. Therefore, in any given short period of time, it is as likely to move against our wishes as it is to please us.

If the market overreacts the wrong way just after one has invested, one has no real problem when one invests on a flexible time schedule. One simply may wait a little longer for the desired change to occur. If one is investing according to a fundamentally derived long-term prediction, and the adverse market response is not because of new information that undermines our evaluation, then one is likely to be on pretty solid ground by waiting.

However, if the investment is limited to a precise period, as say a three-month duration, then one cannot escape the random vicissitudes of market fluctuation. If one "sells short" (that is, if one sells borrowed stock that has to be replaced), one must repurchase the stock within a specific period, for example, ninety days. If one trades in <u>options</u> (puts and calls), one is bound to the option period. If one trades in <u>warrants</u>, without the desire to exercise the warrant, one's time frame is narrowly confined by the life of the warrant. These are obvious ways to bind oneself to a particular time frame and hence lose flexibility and increase risk. An adverse market action in that time period is then transformed from a thing of no real consequence to an irrevocable loss.

Buying stock on <u>margin</u> is a less obvious way to bind oneself to time period. It is less obvious, because one has not contemplated a time period. However, if the stock moves sharply downward, the broker who has extended you the credit may be required to call in the loan and the stock forced into a sale at precisely the wrong time.

This form of risk enlargement is unproductive because there is no <u>investment</u> objective to be gained. One may assume a larger risk by buying lower-rated bonds because the consequent interest is higher. To do this is to accept a higher risk for a clear investment objective. However, the advantage of this kind of risk (margins, options, warrants, etc.) is only leverage, increasing the amplitude of movement, either up or down. This is basically gambling rather than investing. Furthermore, with (1) commissions on all transactions, whether profitable or not, and (2) the possible time trap, the odds for this gamble are stacked against the speculator. Only two persons can prudently enter such waters: (1) those who possesses special firsthand knowledge and (2) those who are hedging against the opposing risk that circumstances have cast.

Fixed Time and Lost Flexibility

Certain forms of investment require that they be maintained for a specified period of time. Certificates of deposit and "money market funds" offered by banks or savings and loan associations may specify times ranging from three months to three years. If one knows that one will not want the money until the end of that time period, then this may be a convenient form of investment. For example, if one knows of a sum that will have to be paid in just three years, then a three-year commitment is both prudent and convenient.

However, if one's personal timetable does not coincide with the fixed period of the investment, then one may have unwittingly forfeited opportunities or increased the risk of loss. A cash reserve is not truly a cash reserve if it cannot be called upon when needed. Unexpected needs, like hospital bills, will then have to come from disinvesting at a time that may be unfortunate and entail accepting a penalty or selling instruments at a market bottom.

Market conditions may undergo great changes, introducing a profusion of new opportunities for profitable investment, as the stock market in 1932, 1974, or 1982. If one's "reserves" were time bound, one might be unable or unwilling to take the opportunities. A prudent investor ought to have a reserve for contingencies. That reserve is only a masquerade if it is not flexible enough to be used when it's wanted.

Bonds and Length of Time to Maturity

There are two distinct and opposite relationships between length of time to maturity and risk of loss with bonds. The longer the maturity, the greater is the risk to principal, but the less the risk to income. If a bond with one year remaining until maturity is bought at a yield of 15%, this yield can be counted on for only one year. If interest rates drop, next year's replacement may provide a lower yield. However, a thirty-year bond will continue to provide the current owner with the same yield to maturity for thirty years. Therefore, high-current interest rates are protected by buying long maturities.

However, the risk to principal grows greater with increasing maturity. There are two reasons for this increasing risk. First, the longer the maturity, the more likely one will have to sell the issue on the open market, thereby experiencing the impact on market price that a change in interest rates brings. If one holds a bond with only three months left, should interest rates rise sharply and bond prices accordingly drop, one may simply hold the issue until it matures, avoiding any loss to principal. The longer the term to maturity, the greater the likelihood that circumstances will force a market sale. Second, prices of long-term issues react more strongly to interest rate changes as described earlier.

Chapter 7

Benefits

To get the most benefit from your investments, know the forms in which they may arrive. You can do this best with some idea of the underlying sources of benefits. What do the benefits represent? Where do they come from? What stimulates their potential existence? As we understand the source and forms of benefits, we are better able to reap potential benefits and to avoid chasing mirages.

THE CONNECTION BETWEEN RISK AND BENEFIT

It is widely believed that " . . . in general the higher the return the higher the risk involved."[1] Where you find one savings account paying a higher rate of interest, it is probably more risky. One distinguished professional and academic investment expert, Harry Sauvain, maintained that "the way to maximize investment returns is to invest in securities of the lower grades and to assume the larger investment risks insofar as an investor's circumstances permit" (emphasis added to minimize distortion resulting from removal of the quotation from context).[2]

There is much truth to this. If by the size and arrangement of one's portfolio together with the appropriate attitude one has the ability to tolerate a few sour ventures, then one may be limiting returns needlessly by confining investments to issues of the highest quality and least volatility. Sauvain found that "the net returns on securities tend to increase with increasing degrees of financial risk."[3] Poor-quality bonds will yield more than those of good quality. This surplus, it has been argued, is more than sufficient to offset the greater rate of default.

While it is true that larger gains often spring from greater risk, this is not true of all risks. Although true of financial risk and of systematic risk attaching to interest rate fluctuation, it is false about purchasing power risk. A decision to keep all of one's funds in a federally insured bank savings account carries little benefit and assumes a major risk from capital erosion. It is also predominantly false about the risk associated with positive public favor, reflected in overpricing. Here the greater rewards essentially coincide with the least risk: investing at disfavored times or in disfavored issues.

Thus, the validity of the generalization of greater benefits from greater risks is limited to certain risks like financial risk and interest rate risk. Furthermore, even here, its validity depends upon certain conditions. The generalization assumes that the investor has undertaken certain defensive arrangements of the portfolio to limit misfortunes when they occur. The use of proper diversification, an adequate reserve, and other risk-limiting tactics described in chapters 9 and 10 are required. The prudent investor attempts to assess both risks and potential benefits together.

THE SOURCES OF BENEFITS

Within a Time Period

Operating Profit

Importance to Value Orientation

Operating profit is the most basic source of benefits. This is true not only for those who own a share in the profits, namely stockholder, partner, or single proprietor. Interest to creditors, wages and salaries to employees, products to consumers, and taxes to government all depend upon the survival of the enterprise, which requires profits for perpetuation. It is not only the owners of a company who look to its income. A banker considering a loan will regard the income as the primary support. It is axiomatic that bonds are rated primarily in terms of the protection afforded by the issuer's income. Because operating profit is the basic source of benefits, it is crucial to a value-oriented appraisal.

The importance of operating profit has been demonstrated by the tragedies caused by government industries operating by priorities other than profit. Such projects, which have included Egyptian and Indian steel mills, have been compelled to put the profit motive second to other diverse priorities, including the provision of employment, national self-sufficiency, and national prestige. Where these industries have been continued without profit, their operation has resulted in the impoverishment of the citizenry. Without profits, other sources of support are required. Increases in taxes, public deficits, and inflation have been the alternatives.

Amenability to Value-Oriented Use

Determinability

The measure of operating profit is total revenues minus all the expenses required to produce those revenues. Although seemingly straightforward, the allocation of costs and revenues to time periods requires some accounting judgments. At times such judgments have been shaped or abused in order to create a particular image. Possible forms in which earnings per share may be misleadingly reported include the following: (1) the inappropriate exclusion of special charges or gains from ordinary income. Truly special charges are properly segregated in reporting, but this device can be used inappropriately to keep items from inclusion; (2) failure to appropriately clarify an adjustment for dilution. (*Dilution* is the decrease in proportional ownership of each share of stock because of an increase in the number of shares. This may occur from things like the exercise of stock options, the conversion of convertible issues, or the issuance of additional stock to acquire a subsidiary, etc.); and (3) changing accounting methods such as methods of depreciation or assigning inventory to sales.

Since operating profit is one of the central indices of value, do we simply give up trying to apply standards of value, as some contrarians have suggested?[4] Fortunately, we have three safeguards. First, we can avail ourselves of the advisory services' reporting of data. A worthy service will have inspected these figures with some expertise from an unbiased point of view. Second, do not exaggerate the significance of the earnings per share of single time periods. Although the investment community gives great attention to the latest quarterly earning figures, it is most important to regard the flow of earnings across time. If we look across an expanse of time, we are unlikely to be importantly misled by these tactics. Third, if we do rely upon the company's own reporting completely, we can do so with some knowledge of corporate accounting and a reading of appended notes, including those of the auditor. I therefore assert that past and current earnings can be given a satisfactorily approximate measure.

Can we go beyond this to predict future earnings with any accuracy? It is my contention that in some cases, earnings estimates will have a high likelihood of approximate accuracy, and in other cases, estimates are simply guesses. <u>The important point is that we have some power to distinguish those situations where we can estimate accurately from those where we cannot</u>. Thus, if we want to be able to predict with some assurance, we can avoid those areas where we are led to believe that predictions would be hazardous. Simple naive projections from past trends show considerable accuracy in many cases. Arguably, financial analysts can improve upon this, and their improvement can be aided by the use of management's forecasts. Concluding from a study Scott conducted, she says, "If you are using analysts' forecasts, you can be more assured of the accuracy of the earnings estimates for a firm whose management announces its own earnings forecasts . . . . You can also be assured that analysts are making good use of the information they receive and that they are more prone to conservatism and healthy skepticism."[5]

Relationship to Stock Prices

Because I propose that operating profits are the primary basis of value for the stockholder, I must address a viewpoint I saw put forth in the financial pages of a local newspaper. Dohmen-Ramirez claimed that " . . . the stock market is not a function of earnings, but of the amount of money available to buy stocks."[6] Although I agree with two of the points contained or implied within this statement, I strongly disagree with it. First, I agree that the amount of money available has a strong and important effect on the stock market. Liquidity may power a bull market, and tightness of funds may start a bear market. Second, I agree with the implication that the stock market does not move in perfect synchrony with earnings. Indeed, one of the major themes in this book is that myriad factors interfere with and partially obscure a fundamental relation of price to value. Remember that I hold this relationship to assert itself primarily in the <u>long run</u>. In the short run, the market will be pushed randomly by this or that influence, people will function with less-than-perfect rationality, and prices will tower above or sink below an overall normative value. In the long run, the normative value will recur. Yet even in the short run, a change in earnings will normally precede a parallel change in market price.

Therefore, in spite of the two areas of agreement, I differ profoundly with the position that stock market price is not determined by earnings. Dohmen-Ramirez as a president of "a Honolulu-based <u>money-management firm</u>" (emphasis added)[6] pits <u>monetary conditions</u> against earnings on the basis of a study he did, but the details of which he apparently thought inappropriate to present. Let me therefore briefly mention another study. I related corporate earnings to stock prices across the sixty-three-year period from 1920 to 1983, using the average stock prices and earnings per share for the group of companies represented in the Dow Jones average.

If Dohmen-Ramirez's hypothesis were accurate, I should have found no significant relationship. If his implication was correct, though insignificant, I should have found a negative relationship. First, I found a significant, positive, and robust correlation (r = + .87, p < .01) between actual yearly earnings per share and stock prices. Since a correlation of 1.00 represents a perfect or complete relationship, the current .87 is robust and indicates a strong bond. It indicates that 76% ($.87^2$) of the variation in stock prices is reflected in the variations of yearly earnings. The "+" indicates a positive relationship: as earnings advance so do stock prices. The notation "p < .01" means that the odds that the positive correlation might be a quirk of chance are less than 1 in 100. The correlation is therefore regarded as significant.

Second, realizing that the use of total yearly figures might allow a third factor, inflation, to intervene to expand both figures together, thus strengthening the appearance of a relationship, I removed the effect of inflation by the statistical technique of partial correlation. The result was also significant and positive ($r_{12.3}$ = + .58, p < .01). This is an interesting result as it tells us that (a) the relationship between earnings and prices exists in its own right independently of inflation; (b) although reasonably strong, the relationship is usually not apparent ($r^2_{12.3}$ = .33); and (c) significant positive relationships exist between inflation and each of these two: earnings (r = + .89, p < .01) and stock prices (r = + .80, p < .01).

Third, a more stringent test of the relationship between earnings and prices would be to relate yearly changes in one with yearly changes in the other. This is more stringent because it removes slower acting aspects of a relationship. Both anticipatory and historical effects are eliminated. Nevertheless, the result was that again, a significant positive correlation was found (r = + .33, p < .01). Note that with the time linkage arbitrarily shortened, the connection, although attenuated, still exists.

Finally, my assertion that earnings or operating profits are the primary basis of value for the stockholder places me in enormously broad company, which includes many notables. Benjamin Graham, along with many others, calculates stock values by a formula involving a multiplication of earnings.[7]

Payment for Use

This is the straightforward reimbursement for the temporal use of something. For the use of money, we speak of interest. Rent is payment for the temporal use of tangible property. Wages, salary, or commissions are payments for human services. Where such payment for use is the primary business of the individual or enterprise, then it provides the revenues from which the subtraction of appropriate costs results in operating profits.

Windfall

A windfall is a fortuitous gain resulting from a generally unforeseen and sudden change in the configuration of supply and demand facing an enterprise. Windfalls are likely to be unpredictable except for those with astute foresight or for those who exercise improper influence.

Growth

A General Characteristic of Common Stock

Growth springs from an increase in operating profits across successive time periods. When one buys common stock in a growing company, one has not made just one static investment as one has with a bond or a bar of gold. Beyond this, the stock itself represents ownership of a continually investing enterprise. The typical company retains part of its earnings to inject into new investment opportunities. It may be seeking an expansion of its current area of operation, an improvement of its operation, or the creation of a totally new ancillary enterprise. The result is real new investment. The stockholder as an owner of the enterprise participates in this according to his share of ownership. Owning common stock in such a company, you are continually having new investments made on your behalf. This is the source of growth. If the new investments are successful, growth results.

Growth arises then out of operating profits when a portion of those profits are prudently reinvested. Thus it has two determinants which are the following: (1) the percentage of earnings retained for use by the company (this is also earnings minus dividends) and (2) the profitability of its investments. A figure that expresses both determinants simultaneously is the earnings retained expressed as a percentage of net worth.

Do not think of growth as only a single form of benefit. Do not limit yourself to thinking of it merely as a source of a capital gains. This is because growth is an aspect of the total company's earnings, which may be revealed either in successive increases in dividends, market prices, or both simultaneously. One can choose to take the rewards of growth in gains from increased market value, although the prudent investor may prefer to realize growth in the form of an increasing stream of income. In this manner, the new investments made for the investor escape (1) needless commissions and (2) the taxation that occurs when an investor sells his holding to take a capital gain and reinvest the depleted after-tax proceeds.

It is wrong to think of growth as simply an increase in size or an expansion in output. Of course, this may be the form growth takes, but other forms are possible. If the new investment involves enhancing the productive process by creating more effective means of production, growth may be accompanied by decreases in plant size. Growth may be manifest as increase in safety, job satisfaction for employees, and the introduction of previously unknown products or services.

In 1924, Edgar Smith[8] shook the fashionable concepts of investment of his time with a fascinating study of comparative investments in stocks and bonds over an extended period of time, from 1837 to 1923. Admittedly, the data at his disposal were sketchy, and he was forced to work with multiple samples across overlapping twenty-year spans. Yet even <u>after</u> correcting for the effects of changes in purchasing power of the dollar (which of course favored stocks), Smith found contrary to conventional wisdom that stocks still surpassed bonds in performance. His analysis revealed a long-term secular growth trend of about 2.5% compounded yearly throughout the eighty-six-year period. Note this is in addition to the increase from inflation. He attributed this to the practice of corporate boards of directors of continually reinvesting a portion of surplus earnings. This secular upward trend in stock prices was sufficiently strong that stock market lows were, with only one exception, always higher than the highs of ten years earlier. On that one occasion, it required just over fifteen years for the high to be surpassed by the market low point.

Going from Smith's time to the present is much easier. Value Line computes the <u>average</u> Dow Jones Industrials' earnings growth rate from 1920 to 1997 to have been 5.4% compounded yearly.[9] Over this period, it reports inflation to have averaged 3.0% compounded yearly, so that the adjusted or "real" rate of earnings growth would have been 2.4% (5.4% minus 3%), which is interestingly close to Smith's estimate. To the extent that one can accept Smith's data as widely representative, one is tempted to say that this upward trend in growth has been manifest continually across the past 160 years, the time for which we have data.

In the period since Smith's publication, we have two contrasting extremes, the market boom of the twenties followed by the Great Depression. The market in 1929 was enormously overvalued, while the trough of the depression was accompanied by a protracted undervaluation. In this instance, it required much longer for the cumulative growth to lift stock market <u>lows above the previous 1929 high</u>. The stock market high of 1929 was not bested by a stock market low until 1954, twenty-five years later. That is, never since 1954 has the stock market been as low as the stratospheric height of the heady 1929 boom. Although the Dow Jones in 1929 was at the same level as in 1954, there was an enormous contrast between the two occasions because of the twenty-five years of intervening growth. In 1929, the market was bloated and ready to fall. In 1954, it was lean and poised for a fourteen-year advance.

If 2.6% seems like an insignificantly small amount, keep in mind four things. <u>First</u>, this figure is only the "real" growth. For equities there is also the growth from inflation in which fixed-dollar forms of investment do not participate. <u>Second</u>, as dividends also are being paid, growth is only part of the benefit being received. <u>Third</u>, this is merely the average experience. One ought to improve on this experience since besides recessions, it includes (1) fading and faltering enterprises; (2) a recession prolonged and transformed into a catastrophic depression by the Federal Reserve's tight money policy, an approach that they must surely have learned to avoid in the future. <u>Finally</u>, as calculated, this figure was relentlessly compounding. At 2.6% compounded over a lifetime, we would experience a <u>gain</u> of more than 500%, and a sixfold increase in dividends.

Variability in Growth

As with most things, growth is not a constant. Growth varies between companies. Some companies grow by giant leaps, others less rapidly, still others only slowly, while some falter. Growth between companies varies not only in speed, but also in continuity.

Growth also varies within the same company over time. Growth in companies often resembles the standard growth functions found in nature. Of these we may say the following: (1) if a population expands freely over an unrestricted environment, the percentage rate of increase is constant; (2) however, if it encounters limits, its rate of growth will slow before finally halting. Consider a colony of organisms grown, in a finite or limited space, as bacteria in a culture. When looked at in absolute terms, at first they seem to multiply slowly, then pick up speed, next gradually taper off in speed of growth, and finally reach an asymptote. Beyond this, the colony will not grow without a change in environment.

It must always be remembered that growth is normally limited by the environment and this is always changing for businesses. Markets approach saturation. Strong profits attract competition, which compels adjustments in methods and pricing. Yet like any organism, a business is not merely shaped by its environment, but may have the reciprocal power to shape that environment. The most obvious examples are by creating new products and by advertising.

The pattern of variation in growth within an enterprise differs across companies. Some companies retain the constant rate of growth over long stretches of time, while others quickly blossom and fade. Thus, in selecting a stock for growth, the stability or predictability of growth is pertinent.

The Stigma of Growth Issues or Industries

While the spectrum of rates of growth varies across a wide range, public favoritism in the past has gone to the spectacular issues and industries. They were spectacular either because they exhibited extreme growth or they were poised on the threshold of a new and seemingly limitless domain. As glamour stocks, their prices were bid up to absurdly high levels. Investors buying at those levels eventually had to experience loss and frustration. Thus a stigma arose. However, the stigma attached inappropriately to growth. It would have been more appropriately attached to absurd overvaluation.

The lure of extreme growth will probably continue to lead to insupportably high valuations and their consequent disasters. Yet while the market's attention in the area of growth is riveted on extreme issues, moderately high sustained growth may be ignored.

For example, throughout the five years beginning with 1979, American Home Products was rated by Value Line "1" (the highest) for safety and "A++" (the highest) for financial strength, sold at an average P/E ratio of 10.7 and an average yield of 5.62%. All the while, its earnings and dividends increased each year at a satisfactorily dependable 12% compound rate. That amounts to 76% growth in that five-year span. At that rate, if market price kept pace with earnings growth, which in the long run it tends to do, $100 invested initially would result in $176 in five years, $310 in ten, $547 in fifteen, and $965 in twenty years. Actually, over the sixteen years from 1970 through 1986, its earnings grew 662%.

Yet this leaves aside the dividend that flourished at a similar rate. The stock not only earned more each year, thus becoming more valuable, its dividends burgeoned persistently larger each year. Calculating the current yield on the initial cost gave a measure of dividend growth. A dividend with this initial yield of 5.62%, after ten years of such growth would yield over 17% per year on the initial cost while after fifteen years, the yield would have grown to over 30%, and after twenty years, 54% of cost. On a no-growth instrument, such as a nonconvertible bond or preferred stock, the yield calculated this way would remain the same 5.62% of original cost regardless of the number of years one held the investment.

Historically, one could have purchased American Home Products in 1953 at a yield of 6.3%. Had one done so, one's 1987 yield on that invested cost would have become 340% per year. That is, the dividends received in 1987 would have been 3.4 times the total price paid for the stock in 1953. An investment of $100 then would have had a 1987 market value of $8,400, and in the meantime would have paid $1,969 in dividends. Furthermore, the stock continued to grow, albeit at a slower rate of 9.1% to 1998. This company had increased both earnings per share and dividends in every year since 1953, excepting only 1992 when its earnings held steady. It did this at an average growth rate of more than 11.7% per year maintained over the 44 years for which I have immediately accessible information.

I do not mean to imply by the above that one can be certain that such growth will occur. Being human, we do not know the future. But we can attempt to forecast, and in doing so, we are not without guidelines to tell us how good or bad the forecast is likely to be. However, what I mean to illustrate above is (1) the growth potential exists and (2) that it is to be found much more widely than with today's superstars of growth. Indeed, the more extreme the growth visible today, the less is the likelihood of its continuation.

THE FORMS OF BENEFITS

The primary benefits come in two forms, periodic payments and gains on sales. It may seem natural to associate the forms with the sources of benefit. For example, we might be tempted to link real estate rental value with periodic payments. Yet growth of operating profits affects periodic payments as much as gains on transactions.

There is also a third form of benefit, which I hesitate to name because of (1) its relative unimportance and (2) its potential for mischievous and perverse effect; but, in light of the public ballyhoo, I shall also mention a third form of reward: tax benefits.

Periodic Payments

These are the <u>only</u> form of benefit for some investments such as nonmarketable bonds, certificates of deposit, and savings accounts. They are the <u>principal</u> form of reward for others like short-term bonds and even long-term bonds bought at low yield. They may be the <u>preferred</u> form of benefit for stocks paying out a continually growing stream of dividends and bought on a long-term basis for steadily increasing income.

Most stocks and other ownership investments pay dividends, while bonds and other creditor forms pay interest. In either case, the investor receives or may hope to receive payments periodically to augment or constitute his income. As indicated previously, bondholders have a legal priority, and interest is required to be paid; stockholders are paid only if the directors vote to do so. However, both dividends and interest are normally paid routinely according to an anticipated schedule. Interest on bonds is paid semiannually, while dividends are usually paid each quarter, although some companies pay according to different schedules.

Yield

The yield of a security is the relative size of its current periodic payments. This is calculated by dividing the sum of the payments received in the current year by the price of the instrument and multiplying by 100, so that the yield reflects the percentage of the cost of the security that is returned in payments to the owner in one year. Example Company, whose stock is selling for $100 per share, pays quarterly dividends of $1 per share on the first of March, June, September, and December. A stockholder receives $4 per year on a $100 investment. The yield is 4%.

Yields on securities vary in magnitude across a wide range from 0 to more than 18%. In 1984, the median yield for Value Line's list of stocks was 3.4%. At that rate (assuming no sale, no inflation, no dividend changes, and no reinvestment of dividends), it would have taken 29.4 years to return one's investment. As I write this, average yield of the Dow Jones stocks estimated by www.indexarb.com is now 2.79%. The range is from 6.76% to 0.24%. The Standard and Poor's range is wider.

Usually a lower yield reflects the market's higher evaluation of the security, as people do not want lower-quality issues unless they receive sufficiently more. Variations in yield from one bond to another reflect primarily the public estimate of risk. <u>The greater the perceived risk, the higher the yield</u>.

Thus, a three-month U.S. Treasury bill can be expected to yield less than a thirty-year debenture of a poorly situated corporation. Lower yields on municipals reflect the desirability of the nontaxable status. For a stock, a lower yield could arise not only from the estimate of lower risk. Other benefit features such as expectations of dividend growth or the prospect of capital gains are likely to be persuasive.

In the nineteenth and early twentieth centuries, bonds traditionally provided lower yields than common stocks, reflecting the perception of their lower risk. However, in the 1920s, it was noted that from 1897 on diversified common stocks proved more profitable investments than high-grade bonds. Partly, this reflected the ability of stocks to adjust to inflation. Partly, it reflected an increasingly widespread appreciation of growth as one of the benefits of common stock. Because of these changed perceptions, over the past sixty years yields on common stocks have tended to be lower than those on bonds.

<u>Capital Gains</u>

Source of Gains

"Buy cheap and sell dear" is the age-old formula for this benefit. The excess of the selling price over the buying price (less the expenses of the transactions and of interim maintenance) is the gain on the transaction. The gain (or loss) depends upon the fluctuations in price over a period of time.

To an investor wanting a tip on the market, the fabled J. P. Morgan is supposed to have replied, "It will fluctuate." Morgan gave not only an amusingly evasive reply, but also the most fundamental and valid description of market action. Keep in mind that this portrayal of market action is not valid just for the stock exchange. It also fits the bond market and about anything that we may buy or sell, including gold, commodities, and real estate.

Since gains depend upon price fluctuations across time, are we merely gambling upon the direction of fluctuation when we invest for gain? Is it not just as likely for the fluctuation to go against us, causing a loss? Since fluctuations spring from changing combinations of events, are there any patterns to the fluctuations that would enable us to make better than chance predictions? Let us look at the components of price fluctuation.

Components of Price Fluctuation

<u>Short Term</u>

Very Short Term

The very short term embraces price movements that take place from hour to hour, from day to day, or for as long as one month before imperceptibly merging into the moderately short term. From hour to hour, the input can be seen to be extremely varied. The president might be hospitalized. A favorable or unfavorable economic statistic may be issued. OPEC ministers may reach accord, fail to do so, or adjourn until the morrow. Forces acting on interest rates may push them up or down. A corporate scandal or statistic may be rumored. The United States or an antagonistic power may issue a bellicose statement. Someone in charge of a very large institutional account may succumb to emotional pressures and act erratically. An investment guru may pontificate on the market stampeding investors to buy or sell. There are so many possible sudden inputs or stimuli to stock market action that a lengthy book would be required to catalog them. But the essence of it is that at any moment <u>anything</u> can happen to stimulate the public to buy or to sell. <u>In the very short run, market behavior is random.</u>

The Longer Short Term

This refers to a time span of from two weeks to one year or eighteen months. You notice that this time span overlaps the previous one. One of the difficulties in utilizing what patterns may be found in this time period derives precisely from this temporal uncertainty. In this more protracted short term, trends of limited duration may be retroactively identified. However, antecedent or even concurrent identification of duration, including the time of both onset and cessation, may be quite precarious.

Within this time span, various patterns may emerge for a while. Interest rates may drift in a direction. Public sentiment toward the market as a whole, selected industries, or individual companies may consistently press in a particular direction. Yet, while some short-term tendencies may retroactively seem defined in their systematic impact on the market, the task of concurrently identifying the tendency and the precise period of its duration is sufficiently hazardous as to make it a tool of dubious use for the investor.

Many people have made quite accurate predictions of these market movements for a while. Many of these have been hailed as gurus, only to have subsequently erred so badly as to bring their average performance close to chance expectancy. The random walk hypothesis mentioned earlier suggests that those who attempt to predict short-term market action from market indices themselves will do no better than blind guessing. The situation may be somewhat better for those whose predictions are based upon a study of external antecedent factors. Yet even here the prognosticator is bedeviled with unknowns. For example, having identified the money supply as becoming less tight and knowing this to be bullish, one does not know whether this will continue for a year or reverse itself next week. One is on somewhat firmer ground if one has several independent antecedents that are bullish, since, being independent, it is unlikely they would reverse themselves simultaneously.

However, it is not that easy to find stable antecedent factors. In part, this is because the stock market is itself generally one of the leading economic indicators. Another problem would appear to be that if one could find such a factor and demonstrate that it works, that knowledge alone would change the behavior of the market. We must leave this an open question, which remains to be explored.

Cyclical Variations

National income and production follow a pattern of expansion followed by contraction. Production, employment, income, prices, and profits alternately balloon and deflate. This successive alternation between contraction and expansion has been generally called the business cycle. It has been with us in industrial nations apparently since an interdependent monetary economy replaced one based on barter and self-sufficiency. If one attempted to select a preeminent cause for these cycles, it might well be fluctuations in money supply and net real investment.

Although successive business cycles have many similarities and follow this alternating pattern, their properties and timing are far from identical and their actions accordingly cannot be described by the kind of clean equations that can be used for cycles of moon phases or other natural phenomena. Business "cycles" seem rather to represent a clumsy feedback system endeavoring to correct earlier errors or excesses usually by creating new excesses in the opposite direction.

The average length of a business cycle is a matter of debate. Some count only major cycles and find an average of eight years per cycle. Yet others note two or sometimes even three minor cycles within a major cycle.

The picture is complicated by the observation that cycles are known only by variations across time and that causative economic conditions are also changing with time. It is possible that current cycles are shorter. One fairly safe generalization about cycles is that the more extreme in amplitude they are, the more protracted they are likely to be. It also appears that the more pronounced the excesses during a boom, the deeper will be the succeeding abatement.

Stock market cycles usually reflect business cycles. If one scans for successive obvious stock market lows from 1921 to 1997, one could find fourteen, of which eleven coincide with business cycles. For example, the onset of the Great Depression coincides rather closely with the stock market crash of 1929. Both continued their slide together until 1932, when both began a tentative recovery that peaked in 1937 before descending roughly together to the 1938 trough.

However, if one attempts to use this pattern of cyclical fluctuation in stocks to predict future movements, one runs into several difficulties, including the following:

a. The stock market tends to lead rather than follow other economic measures. As a crude rule of thumb, it has been estimated to anticipate the economy by about six months. It therefore may start to rise while the Index of Industrial Production is falling, or drop while the index is rising.

b. Cycles are not clearly defined phenomena. The greatest agreement on them is reached in retrospect, and even then, disagreement exists. One may suspect that a recession is beginning only to find that it was an unevenness in the progression of an expansion.

c. Cycles differ in their causative factors, the circumstances that stimulate their onset or cessation. The crucial leading indicators on one occasion are not identical to those of another occasion. Excessive interest rates may throttle investment in one period but be unimportant in what discourages investment in another.

d. There are greater differences between companies than between cyclical periods. Companies are affected by the conditions of their industry and by the way they have positioned themselves. Traditionally, capital goods industries, those whose products are sold to other companies to support their functioning, are the most volatile. The machinery and machine tool industries are prime examples. Secondary partial examples are steel and concrete. At the other extreme are companies that have a demand for their products that is <u>inelastic</u> (changes in the price have little effect upon the amount sold). Their output tends to be inexpensive consumer products like tobacco or staple foods.

For these reasons, it is difficult to successfully and consistently "play" the cyclical variations. Doing this in a straightforward way is something best left to those having both the knowledge and willingness to continually scrutinize the economy and the market. Attempting to take advantages of cyclical variations by being advised by those who proclaim themselves experts is, however, not the same as being an expert. Unless you are being advised this way on an individual basis, so probably are thousands of others. Furthermore, your market action will undoubtedly lag behind the promulgation of the advice.

<u>Long-Term Trend</u>

Look at the stock price chart from 1920 to 1997 (fig. 7.1). The most striking feature is the persistent upward trend. As I write this, the Dow has continued to move up and is now at 10,997.35, some 2,900 points higher than the chart's apex. In spite of reverses and plateaus, a trend line drawn to reflect average stock prices from 1920 to 1997 rises at a relentlessly compounding rate of 6% per year. The visual impact of the upward trend in stock prices over this period dwarfs even the effect of the Great Depression on stock prices. However, even more striking is the more consistently persistent upward trend in common stock earnings (fig. 7.2). This, of course, is powered by two factors, which are (1) growth and (2) inflation.

In spite of the overall robust upward trend of stocks, variations between industries and companies are of overshadowing importance. Some stocks show a clear and consistent upward trend with each successive year being an all-time record. The yearly succession of earnings of other companies is so erratic that no trend is visible even across fifteen years. Some companies show a deteriorating trend. In looking at a stock's long-term trend, one should consider trend direction, magnitude, and predictability.

Fig. 7.1 DJIA AVERAGE PRICES 1920-1997[9]

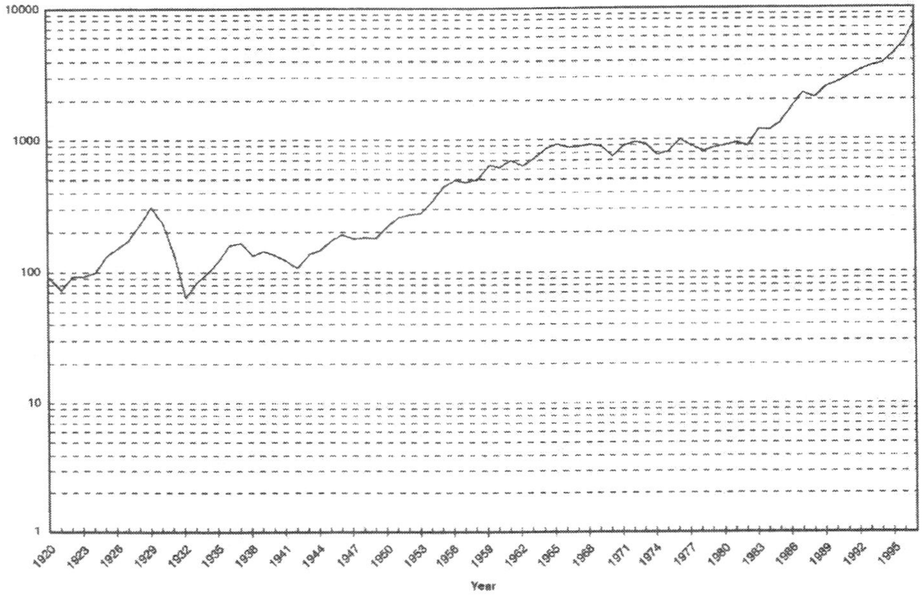

Predictability of Components

This look at the components of price fluctuation leads to a startling hypothesis: the least predictable period is the immediate short-term future, the most predictable is the future stretching out indefinitely from five to twenty years. You are better able to predict market changes five to ten years from now than tomorrow.

A model constructed in accordance with the view of the components of fluctuation presented here illustrated the greater error of the short-term prediction. The particular model assumed random short-term fluctuations, variable cycles (whose length and position were randomly selected), and a secular trend, all combined and extended together across twenty years. Predictions were based on knowledge of nonrandom components. The average error of prediction over the last three years (years eighteen, nineteen, and twenty) was just over 2% while that for the first three years was 291%.

Fig. 7.1 DJIA Yearly Earnings Per Share[9]

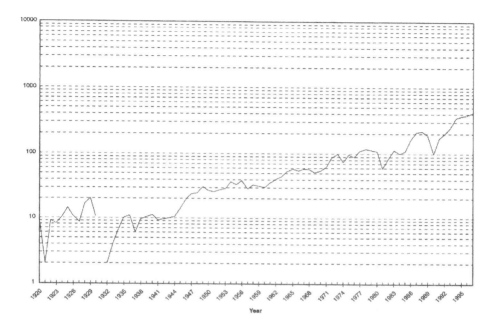

Fig. 7.2 Negative earnings of -0.5 in 1932 is replaced by a gap instead of being shown.

Not surprisingly, the maximum quarterly error occurred in the second quarter of year 1 when an error of 520% was reached. (The error here was calculated as a deviation of the actual change from the predicted change expressed as a percentage of the predicted change.)

However, this illustrative model is limited by its assumptions and can be illustrative but not convincing. Can we really predict the price changes that occur over the next ten years with greater accuracy than tomorrow's? Does this hypothesis not flout common sense and reason? Perhaps the following observations will alter what we think reason tells us:

1. The future is unknowable. This is equally true of tomorrow and ten years from tomorrow. All human beings can do is make error-prone predictions based upon what the past and the present reveal.

2. The predictions we are concerned about are <u>not about total magnitude</u>. Instead, we want to know about the <u>magnitude of changes</u>. When investing

today to sell tomorrow, the measure of profit is the <u>change</u> in price that occurs by tomorrow. Tomorrow's actual total price is meaningless, except insofar as it reveals the change.

The advantage of immediacy gained in predicting to the short term is the greater probable resemblance to today. Yet this concerns totalities, not changes. If I want to predict tomorrow's price for a particular security, my best prediction (without the knowledge of an insider or manipulator) is simply today's price. This is the advantage that immediacy of future prediction confers. However, that is not what I wish to predict. Instead, I am only interested in the difference between today and tomorrow. For although this prediction of total magnitude is more accurate, it can predicate no meaningful investment. Gains and losses are determined by changes, and change, therefore, is what I wish to predict. <u>The predictive advantage conveyed by immediacy is irrelevant to the prediction we wish to make</u>.

3. Very short-term price changes are very strongly biased by chance or random events. Chance refers to a situation where the determinants are too numerous and complex for us to rule out any of the possible outcomes. Tonight the president may have a heart attack, a threat of war may occur, banks may announce a rise in interest rates, the chairman of the Federal Reserve may make a speech, a corporate scandal may be brought to light, the Bureau of Labor Statistics may issue a surprising statistic, an accountant may compile new corporate profit estimates, rumors of a new discovery may circulate, a speech may instill fears in investors, and so forth. These sorts of unpredictable events of tonight will affect tomorrow's price changes.

However, time presents new influences to blunt and offset tomorrow's influences. It is in the long run that most of these unpredictable and mostly extrinsic factors cancel themselves out. It is in the long run that the intrinsic, fundamental, and more predictable factors, corporate earnings trends and long-term norms of value, reveal their impact. A warning, unfortunately, is in order. Note that I said *most* of these unpredictable factors cancel out. Among these unpredictable factors <u>may</u> be some that introduce a change in long-term fundamental patterns. The long-term investor should be aware of this. Although the long-term fundamental patterns of earnings and standards of value provide us with the most well-defined and stable basis for prediction, they must be regarded as subject to change, and hence as our best but nevertheless tentative hypotheses.

Tax Benefits

Some investments provide benefits that are totally or partially exempt from taxation. Others provide the investor with tax deductions, which exceed the benefits paid to the investor, so that not only those benefits may be excluded from taxation; but, in addition, other income of the investor may be sheltered as well.

Before simply assuming that these represent juicy plums waiting to be picked, four observations are in order. First, tax revisions can reverse advantages, thereby possibly creating losses. Second, tax revisions have removed the most flagrant special advantages, the real estate write-offs used notoriously by partnerships created precisely for this purpose of creating a shelter over the investor's other income.

Third, investment markets are not completely blind to value. If a particular issue has an obvious additional value, this is likely to be reflected in the price at which it sells. Interest on some state and local bonds is not taxable by the federal government. It is not terribly surprising to see that such issue accordingly sell at lower yields than taxable issues of comparable safety. For someone in a 28% surtax bracket, a nontaxable issue yielding 3.6% is not better than a taxable issue at 5%. For someone in a 15% bracket, it is worse. The only beneficiaries of this tax break are primarily the local governments and their citizens who have a smaller interest burden to bear and, secondarily, individuals whose ordinary income is taxed at appreciably higher than average rates.

A fourth observation is that the tax advantage may spring from and reflect a deterioration in value. Several common stocks, particularly among the utilities, pay dividends that are partially or sometimes wholly tax-exempt. In these instances, the company is paying out more money than it has earned in the period, so that a portion represents a return of capital rather than income. In such a situation, the stockholder is disinvesting or cashing out his investment. Such tax-exempt dividends are a true boon to the investor only when they result from losses that in actuality belong elsewhere in time or company, but are being recognized for tax purposes here and now.

Only in those situations where the tax laws permit either (1) a postponement of taxability or (2) a formal recognition of deterioration in value that is not actually occurring can a special benefit truly be conferred to the business. Moreover, it is not always clear that a tax advantage for a business means an equivalent advantage to the owners. Economic factors will determine the division of advantage between owners, employees, and customers.

Tax benefits arising from the ability to postpone taxability are associated with retirement funds. For the stockholders, they also attach to the retention and reinvestment of corporate earnings. In both of these cases, the postponement allows funds to grow more rapidly than would otherwise be possible.

PART FOUR

TAKING ACTION

Chapter 8

Strategy

From here on, I tilt toward more advocacy and less exposition. Heretofore, my intention has been to present a panoramic view of investments, with their instruments, institutions, risks, and benefits, as well as of investors with their strengths, vulnerabilities, and objectives. Where you will have noticed advocacy, it has occurred within the context of exposition. Now we come to the principles of action that I espouse. I advance these for the prudent individual who wishes to enhance growth and income to the extent consistent with safeguarding his or her savings. I have no wish to burden you or myself by cataloging all possible strategies. I hope that if your objectives differ, you will nonetheless be able to use my presentation to attune strategy and tactics suited to your own ends. Therefore, beginning with this chapter on strategy, I shall be speaking of those principles of action that in my judgment are important for the investor who is primarily interested in pursuits other than investments, has little spare time, and yet who wishes to preserve and enlarge his savings and income.

FUNDAMENTAL VALUE ORIENTATION

I submit that it is fundamentally important, in investments as elsewhere, to seek out, recognize, and cleave to enduring basic value. Although this may sound trite and vacuous, I am in fact advocating the willful choice of a specific unpopular alternative. I say unpopular because investors practice it with the frequency that fish soar through the air. Even among those giving lip service to fundamental value, many surreptitiously or unknowingly interject incompatible overriding priorities.

The conventional investment strategy is to maximize favorable market action in the immediate future. This requires correctly anticipating what other people will be doing next week or next month. Concern is absorbed in predicting fashionable trends—blind to intrinsic value. When observed overtime practitioners of this strategy demonstrate two major results: (1) a meager ability to predict such trends accurately and (2) the lunacy of the possible resulting positions.

The stock market in 1929, as on other occasions like 1972, illustrated how one can thrust oneself over a financial precipice by riding market trends while blithely ignoring underlying value. In The New Contrarian Investment Strategy, David Dreman colorfully portrays the appalling inability of even professionals to predict market action.[1] The absurd extremities to which people have gone following this market orientation is pungently illustrated by Dreman's descriptions of historical ventures.[2] In the "Mississippi Scheme," a French company offering the lure of wealth from the new world skyrocketed in price until after four years, the market price of its shares was worth eighty times all the gold and silver in France. The absence of corresponding underlying value was obscured by fascination with the rapid upward acceleration.

Nevertheless, the proper antidote to the irrational market behavior of investors is not to detect the current and swim against it. This runs the risk of the same absurdities being reached from another direction. As elaborated earlier, the characterization of human functioning as either totally rational or irrational is in serious error. To reflexively act counter to the general crowd runs the risk that at times they may be acting appropriately.

I propose that we put aside the preoccupation with what everyone else is doing. To reflexively follow or oppose popular fashion is to discard our own capacity for independent assessment and choice. Being aware that we are subject to error, we can adopt safeguards to minimize this tendency to err and then venture to conceptualize, identify, and pursue basic value.

Identifying real value may be difficult because we necessarily deal with appearances, yet the task is not hopeless, as some skeptics insist. Contrary to what some contrarians have implied, pursuing basic value is likely to be far easier in investing than in other areas of life because of the greater clarity and ease of quantification of the relevant value.

Conceptualization of Basic Value

Source of Benefits

The benefits of an investment, whether received in the form of a gain on resale or in periodic payments, derive ultimately from the richness of the thing in which we have invested. "Richness" refers here both to the quality and extent of existing assets and to the potential to generate future wealth.

Some disagree, arguing that the payment that provides gain on resale comes not from the investment itself but from an independent buyer. Extreme advocates of this position espouse the "greater fool theory of value," according to which market action is all that counts and it is determined whimsically by fools who will apply absolutely no yardstick of value whatsoever. Accordingly, the price you pay is of no consequence, because an even greater fool will appear to pay an even more absurd price. Though this may at times seem to be true, given enough time, reality will eventually override wishful thinking to provide a correction.

Events just prior to the stock market collapse of 1929 or the bursting of the South Sea Land bubble or many other similar extravagances may have suggested the truth of the greater fool theory or the irrelevance of intrinsic value. However delayed in these instances, the reality of inadequate underlying value eventually toppled excessive market prices in spectacular crashes.

Conversely, increasing underlying value must eventually prevail over market panic, phobia, or fashionable disdain. In 1981, the Dillingham Corporation, selling at about $17 per share, was able to spin off and transfer to its stockholders $20 per share of its real estate holdings while afterward continuing to retain the $17 per share market value. The spate of corporate takeovers or purchase of other corporations in the early 1980s would not have occurred without underlying wealth inadequately recognized by market valuations.

Market price will tend to fluctuate around a normative valuation of intrinsic worth. At times, market forces will be gripped by panic or mesmerized by the lure of quick gain. When strengthened by the pressure of conformity, market valuations may be pushed to extremes, but eventually, reality will intrude to force a correction. The greater the deviation from underlying value, the more extreme the correction. In the long run, the price will tend to reflect the intrinsic value of the investment.

Reasonable Cost

What we seek from an investment is the perpetuation and enhancement of real wealth. Since in making an investment we are expending wealth in order to secure wealth, we must be concerned with the relationship of the wealth spent to the prospect of wealth returned. Although implicit in the discussion of basic value, the role of cost deserves explicit attention, not only because of its importance, but also because it is so frequently treated with cavalier disregard.

If we determine that the common stock of General Hotcakes Corporation is a great buy at today's price, we cannot assume that it will be a good buy at any future price, regardless of how rapid its sales and growth. The price we pay should be advantageously related to our estimate of the prospective benefits. Those who in 1972 bought glamour stocks at prices greater than sixty times the earnings, or who bought the stock of plodding enterprises at nineteen times the earnings, had an opportunity to learn at first hand that the price paid should be appropriate.

Indices of Basic Value

Intrinsic Earning Power

The ability to earn or produce value is the most important aspect of an investment. Earnings are the usual and appropriate source for the payment of dividends and interest. The importance of earning power reaches beyond this to the protection of the principal invested. Although obvious for stock, earnings also provide the primary protection for corporate bondholders, even those secured by a mortgage. For a railroad bondholder, a claim on unused track is not as comforting as the railroad's uninterrupted operating profits. Moreover, operating profits are the primary protection of employees and customers; an advantageous contract or market position in relation to an insolvent company is of little use. Even savings accounts are more importantly protected by the profitability of the bank than by the assets in reserve.

Real estate is another type of investment importantly valued for its generativity. Land can grow crops or provide a location for commercial, industrial, residential, or recreational use.

The ability to marshal value is also relevant to government securities. Although here (aside from revenue-producing government projects), the conception of increase shifts away from generativity, or creation of value, to the transfer or confiscation of value. Here the appropriate indices of productivity are to be sought in the public tolerance for taxation, inflation, or debt.

The only reliable source of real growth is generativity, or ability to produce value. It is true that market action can increase the price commanded by an investment, but without underlying growth, any such market action has only a purely psychological basis. Gold, for example, may increase in price, but the determinants for a rise, unless arising from the discovery of new uses for gold, are chiefly psychological, and their operation may accordingly appear whimsical.

Measures of Earnings Value

The primary measure of earning power for corporate securities is net earnings. The prospective purchase of bonds will be interested in the coverage they provide for interest payments as indicated by earnings divided by the required interest payments. The basic measure for the common stockholders is the earnings per share of common stock, which is net earnings divided by the number of shares of common stock issued. To minimize temporal distortion, the above measures should be viewed as yearly figures and placed in the context of a span of several years.

The price of a stock divided by its current earnings per share, the price/earnings ratio (P/E), is the conventional measure used to relate the stock's price to its power to generate earnings. A P/E of 10, therefore, means that the price of the stock is ten times greater than its current earnings. Investors have sometimes used a P/E of 10 as a general approximation to an appropriate norm for a stock of average quality and prospects. The Dow Jones stocks are usually above normal quality. Their P/Es tend to vary between 10 and 15. Across the 77 years from 1920 to 1987, the average P/E of Dow Jones stocks has been 13.9; the range was a high of 34.8 to a low in 1979 of 6.8. In March 2010, it was above 16.

Obviously, the deviation of a P/E of a particular stock from the average P/E prevailing at that time will be influenced by the public perception of its qualities. In 1984, the P/E ratios of the stocks covered by Value Line ranged from a high of 86.7 for Aileen Inc. to a low of 2.0 for Long Island Lighting. Then, in 1998, the laurels have passed to Identix Inc. at 90 and Vesta Insurance at 4.9. It should be noted that stratospheric P/Es may result from a sudden sharp drop in earnings more than public favor. Aileen Inc. has disappeared from the listing, while Long Island Lighting rebounded strongly to a P/E of 10.2 in 1997, before being purchased in 1998. P/Es will be elevated by perception of growth potential, anticipated windfall, amplitude of dividend payments, and secure quality. P/Es will be lowered by perception of danger. The most notable effects are the increases for growth and decreases for danger.

Average P/Es of stocks vary across time. At the market low of 1974, the median P/E of all Value Line Stocks with earnings was 4.8. Then, in 1998, it was up to 18.4. The Value Line Industrial Composite of 600 stocks has had an average annual P/E of 14.2 over the twenty-three years before 1986, while ranging from a high of 20.1 to a low of 6.7. This variation depends largely on the general perception of the immediate outlook for stock prices and on the availability of money. The latter is indicated by interest rates (the lower the prevalent interest rates, the greater the availability of money). The former is determined by estimates of short-term corporate earnings, changes in interest rates, attractiveness of alternative investment markets, and the relative strengths of the attitudes of optimism versus pessimism.

The problem of determining how much higher a P/E deserves to be increased because of growth potential has not been satisfactorily solved. I prefer to use not growth alone, but the total of anticipated earnings growth added together with yield. This represents total expected benefits. I feel it is advantageous to adjust for the reciprocal nature of current yield and growth. The ratio I have designed for this purpose is called C for cost and is calculated by dividing the P/E by the sum of the yield plus the expected growth rate. For example, a company having a P/E of 10, yielding 3.5%, and expected to grow at 6.5% per year would have a C of 1 (10 ÷ (3.5 + 6.5)). For a top-quality stock with a fairly predictable earnings growth rate, a C of .75 is very attractively priced, a C of 1.25 is fully priced, while a C exceeding 1.75 is significantly overpriced. These benchmark levels have been derived, with slight adjustments for conservatism and convenience, from a calculation of Cs for the Dow Jones and the Value Line Industrial Composite from average annual index figures. The upper and lower figures are approximately one standard deviation above and below the mean respectively.

Absolute Value Estimates Based on Generativity

P/E ratios and other ancillary ratios such as my C ratio provide guidelines for estimating the appropriateness of price in relation to the underlying earnings power. With adjustments for variations in quality, these ratios provide a means of estimating value by reference to long-term market norms.

Assuming the continuation of past long-term market norms, the above ratios may be all we need to keep us in touch with underlying value. However, some formulas have been developed to measure the absolute value of stocks based upon generativity. Since these require very specific assumptions about the future, they must contain some unknown and possibly major error. Yet they do provide another interesting way of estimating value and may help to throw light on the appropriateness of our normatively derived estimates.

Discounted Future Receipts

This method adds up the present value of all future dividend payments together with a final sale price over a long-term period like twenty years. The present value is determined by discounting the estimated future payments by an interest rate deemed minimally acceptable. Thus, if General Example Inc. paid current annual dividends of $1.00 per share and was estimated to grow at a rate of 10% per year, its dividends would be estimated to be $1.00 this year, $1.10 next year, $1.21 the following year, and so forth for the next twenty years. If we require an 8% return, we would discount these future receipts by 8%. When we discount at 8%, we are saying that a dollar to be received next year is worth only ¢92 today. This year's General Example Inc. dividend payment belongs to year 0 and is not discounted, so its present value is therefore $1.00. Next year's payment is estimated to be $1.10 and must be discounted by 8% (have 8% of its value subtracted) over one year, which results in a present value of $1.01. The following year's dividend at $1.21 would be discounted over two years resulting in a present value of $1.02.

One can then estimate the possible sale price that might be commanded by the stock of General Example Inc. twenty years from now. If our estimate of growth has been on target, the dividend after twenty years would be $6.73. We can then capitalize (compute the value of the principal from its payments) this dividend to obtain a price. We could use the current capitalization rate, a market average capitalization rate, or we could be conservative and assume a rate for a deteriorated company, such as one priced to yield 7.5% in an average year. To yield 7.5%, the dividend would be capitalized at (multiplied by) 13.33. The $6.73 dividend times 13.33 gives a residual value of $89.73 for the stock twenty years from now. Discounted at 8% per year, this results in a present value of the residual value of $16.93. The present value of the stock then is obtained by adding up the present value of the dividends across the twenty years together with the present value of the residual price.

The major difficulty with this approach is the accuracy of our estimate. We can attempt to err on the side of conservatism by making adjustments such as assuming that our growth rate will undergo a decay until it reaches the broad average growth rate for stocks. But even so, we are left with the possibility of error that is compounding across several years.

We can cope with this possibility of error in three ways. <u>First</u>, use this method only in those cases where the consistency of growth rate is sufficiently stable to allow us to have some degree of confidence in our estimate. <u>Second</u>, treat the estimate not as a final statement of value, but rather as an estimate that may reveal potential. <u>Third</u>, make several estimates of value by divergent methods and be guided by the total picture. If all absolute value estimates of a stock we are interested in are greatly inferior to its market price, there is indeed reason for skeptical scrutiny.

Along with other indices of value, I personally use three discounted future receipt values, each computed with somewhat different assumptions. For them I use six different estimates of earnings growth, three derived from Value Line's published projections, and three that I calculate across various periods of the past sixteen years. These are modified downward by defects in financial stability, predictability of growth, and so forth. For one of the values in addition to calculating the earnings growth rate, I calculate the earnings growth rate trend. That is, I compute the tendency of that rate to increase, remain stable, or decline, and combine the rate with the trend in projecting earnings. For another, I make projections on average and on minimal rates of growth modified as indicated above. For conservatism, I introduce a deterioration in growth rates after ten years, each value having a different assumption as to deterioration. Though this may sound like a lot of work, one needs only to make up a spreadsheet to do all of the calculation and then merely plug in the data for the particular company.

The Earnings Multiplier Model

These models essentially apply a normative P/E ratio. They follow the general formula $V = E \times M$ where V = value, E = earnings, and M represents an appropriate multiplier. Benjamin Graham initially proposed that $V = E \times (8.5 + 2G)$ where G represents annual earnings growth expressed as a percentage. [3] I like his incorporation of growth within the multiplier, but $8.5 + 2 \times$ growth strikes me as arbitrary and an excessive premium for growth. Indeed, Graham later implies that growth stocks are not promising investments, a conclusion that may partly follow from this insupportable valuation, but mainly is because high growth stocks tend to be popular and hence overpriced. Graham, noting that stock valuations are not independent of interest rates, later multiplied the above formula by the following adjustment for interest rates: 4.4 divided by 100 times the Aaa corporate bond rate. Thus, if the specified interest rate is 7%, the original formula is cut down by a multiplier slightly less than .63. I include this formula as one of my several value indices of value.

Sharp[4] proposed that a valuation model accommodates itself to current investment conditions. Observing the stock market's response to rates of interest and inflation, he concluded these should be integrated into the model. Sharp obtained normative data from a multiple regression study of Dow Jones levels, earnings, inflation, and P/E ratios. Rounding off the results of that study, Sharp proposes that $V = (E \times beta \times 100) \div (I + 3)$. I represents the inflation rate, and I+3 represents what he calls a "risk-free" interest rate. Beta is introduced as an approximation to the growth rate.

Beta is actually a measure of relative volatility of market price, with average volatility expressed as 1.00. While growth and beta do indeed correlate, it is my general impression that this correlation is carried mostly by the extremes. That is, extremely rapidly growing stocks have volatile prices and nongrowing stocks have steadier prices. It is possible to find stocks growing at significantly above average rates with below average betas; in the early 1980s for example, Dun & Bradstreet was growing at 16.5% with a beta of .90; Harland Industries growing at 17.5% with a beta of .95; and Philip Morris growing at 15% with a beta of .85. I am concerned about this because it is precisely those exceptional stocks with a reasonably high growth rate and a low beta that I find most promising. This type of stock (not specifically the three named, two of which show a slackening of growth) are the more predictable and safer avenues of growth. Beta is, after all, a measure of relative systematic risk. Therefore, I prefer to use an estimate of growth directly instead of beta. Accordingly, I adjust this model to $V = (E \times G \times 10) \div (I + 3)$, where G represents growth expressed as a percentage.

Congruence of Valuation Models

As the stock values we are attempting to assess with these measures are subject to change, the determination of their reliability and validity become tenuous. A study of the measures' agreement with each other provides some insight into both reliability and validity. Clearly, without congruence, we know neither what nor whether we are measuring. The table below shows the current intercorrelations of the six valuation measures I use across 25 stocks:

Table 8.1 Intercorrelation of Valuation Models

	Graham Val	Sharp Value 1	C	DFR4	DFR2	DFR3
Graham Val		0.95	0.97	0.95	0.31	-0.10
Sharp Value 1	0.95		0.91	0.41	0.30	-0.14
C	0.97	0.91		0.60	0.45	-0.01
DFR4	0.95	0.41	0.60		0.98	0.95
DFR2	0.31	0.30	0.45	0.98		0.64
DFR3	-0.10	-0.14	-0.01	0.95	0.64	
MEAN	0.62	0.49	0.58	0.78	0.54	0.27
LEGEND:		$p < 0.01$				
		$p < .05$		DFR is:		
			Discounted Future Receipts			

There are three discounted future receipt models and three earnings growth multiplier models. The strongest single measure here is DFR4, which incorporates the trend of earnings growth alterations. It relates significantly to each of the others. It is followed by Graham's model and next by my C ratio.

Although the discounted future receipts models and earnings growth multiplier models are in general agreement, they give somewhat different patterns. This is good. The generally strong agreement (except for DFR3, which incorporates a pattern of sharp deterioration of earnings growth) allows us to have some confidence that we can conceptualize value in a consistent manner even when using divergent points of view. The model labeled Sharp Value 1 is my modification of this model. Across a partially different and larger pool of stock years earlier, it yielded a significant ($p < .01$) coefficient of correlation of +.91 with DFR2. At that time C correlated +.67 ($p < .01$) with DFR2 and +.39 ($p < .05$) with Sharp Value 1. These findings reflect their commonality: they all are concerned with similar estimates of growth and two are also concerned with the same dividends. Yet there are real differences in treatment, and this is an encouraging beginning to rebut those who deny that value can be meaningfully estimated. Such a rebuttal must await validity measures, which are not quite so easily generated.

Two qualifications of these positive findings are in order. First, estimates of growth were made by the same person (although the growth estimate used in the discounted receipt model undergoes a progressively increasing decay from year 10 to 20). Second, the sample of stocks over which agreement was found all conform to my recommended selection criteria.

Nevertheless, the divergence in the models renders these findings more useful and interesting. By simultaneously using value measures derived from different points of view, we can obtain more information. For a specific stock, concord can lend greater confidence to our estimate; discord can illuminate the assumptions critical to our optimism or pessimism.

Asset Value

Valuation based on assets is normally of secondary importance to valuation by earnings, since in a going concern an asset's worth is reflected by its contribution to operations. However, there are times when it is appropriate to directly look at asset valuation. The most obvious situation is with a company undergoing liquidation. Another instance is of a company with extensive value tied up with nonproductive or underproductive assets that could be sold or transferred to a more productive use. For example, a company with large idle land holdings or natural resources kept in reserve.

For the lay outsider, the estimate of value based upon assets is somewhat more perilous than estimating value from earnings. In addition to the problem of measuring asset value is the uncertainty over when, if ever, the asset values will benefit the investor. The traditional measure of asset value is book value per share, which is the total net worth divided by the number of outstanding shares. However, this represents historical costs rather than current market values. Therefore, for a serious asset valuation approach, a great deal of adjustment may be required. When, however, the preponderance of the value rests upon fairly marketable assets or cash, the problem of valuation may be minimized. The primary use of this approach to valuation, though, I would leave to those who are both diligent and patient.

LONG-TERM PERSPECTIVE

Importance

Only in the long run is market value presumed to reflect normative intrinsic value. Market value must be expected to deviate from normative value for periods of time. It therefore follows that if one is to employ a fundamental value orientation, one should also maintain a long-term perspective.

A long-term outlook is recommended not only because it is indispensable for a fundamental value approach; but, as we have seen earlier, it gives the best basis for making valid predictions. The long run is where we can have the most confidence in our judgments.

Criteria

To qualify as a long-run perspective, our outlook must satisfy the following two standards: length of time and variability of time.

Length of Time

We must not think that market prices will conform to our expectations tomorrow, or even by next year. A time span of up to fifteen years is more appropriate. Fifteen years is a decidedly long estimate of the long-term. Only once in the past eighty-five years has the market's long-term trend required more than fifteen years to overcome the effects of short—and intermediate-term extremity of fluctuation. That one occasion involved the Great Depression, followed by the price controls of World War II and the ensuing postwar expectation of recession. A five-year interval between points of agreement of fundamental value and general market prices is more common.

Variability of Required Time

The second standard is acceptance of the variable or indefinite nature of the required time. We cannot expect that fifteen years from today, our prediction will be validated. Rather, we may have some confidence that at some time or times between now and fifteen years hence our predictions will be validated.

Although this approach requires patience, if we do indeed adopt it, we will be repaid with both results and equanimity. We are not upset to see market prices go down, because first, we have expected this to happen, and second, we have positioned our investments so as to minimize the likelihood of sustaining a real loss because of a market reversal. Our investments are arranged so that we can almost entirely dictate the time of purchase and sale rather than have that time dictated by events beyond our control.

This is no more than we do when we buy a home in which we wish to live and can afford. Since we envision staying indefinitely, it need not bother us if real estate values plummet as long as we are not forced to move. Indeed, we are not even aware that the market value of our home fluctuates daily.

Enabling Position

Reserves

To maintain this long-term stance requires several things. Sufficient cash or income reserves are needed. The money put in long-term investments must not also be expected to meet tomorrow's cash requirements. If insufficient reserves are maintained, one is investing in the short-term. Yet, note that sufficiency is relative to cash demands. Absolute size of reserves does not determine sufficiency. Limited available cash may be transformed into a sufficient reserve by adopting a more modest style of expenditure.

Autonomy

Maintaining a long-term stance also requires that one eschews investment mechanisms that place or may place limitations on the length of time a position may be held. Therefore, buying on margin is inappropriate, because market circumstances can supplant your judgment in determining time and hence price of sale. Investing in warrants or options is out, except where they may be used as a hedge. Short sales likewise bind one to the short term.

MULTIVARIATE APPROACH

Sound investing involves configuration and balance. Although the thought that "the future will see an incredible expansion of robotics" may be true, to invest in robotics with no further thought courts disaster. Taking any approach to investing that looks at only one variable is to blind oneself.

At the most rudimentary level, a sound investment should look at the balance between fundamental value and market price. Huge fundamental value should not blind us to even more immense market price. We must have some idea of the appropriate relationship between the two.

Furthermore, estimates of fundamental value should rest upon a configuration of attributes, with each attribute given its proper weight. To look only at either current earnings, or rapidity of growth, or yield, or safety of principal without taking into account the others is to place oneself in an unknown position. Earnings, growth, yield, predictability, financial strength, volatility, and public effect of operations must all be included together if we are to select an investment that reflects our wishes and values.

One of the reasons for the use of summary formulas of value is that they force us to relate different attributes of an investment. For example, my C ratio, by dividing the P/E ratio by the sum of yield and rate of growth forces a summary integration of earnings, price, growth, and yield. Likewise, the use of a valuation formula based on discounted future dividends requires an integration of the variables used in the formula. For my valuation formulas, this includes dividends, predictability of earnings, rate of growth, consistency of rate of growth, trend of rate of growth, safety, and financial strength, together with a normative concept of acceptable interest. Value Lines statistics on a company will provide these measures.

However, an investor's thoughts should go beyond simple summary formulas. Selection of an issue for investment or sale should rest upon a specific group of criteria. Application of the criteria may be made successively, and only those issues are selected that reflect the proper balance of the various attributes desired.

ACCEPTANCE OF FALLIBILITY

The presumption of infallibility in any phase of life generates unmitigated extremism. This is the fertile ground that nurtures folly, madness, and unbounded devastation. While folly in the sphere of investments may be preferable to elsewhere, it is not something to be courted.

It should be clear that no one is omniscient. Few would dispute this in the abstract. However, once caught in the grip of a vision of the future or of ultimate reality, the doctrinaire authoritarian may sweep away all doubts. Faith, masquerading as knowledge, leaps confidently into the unknown. As the Stanford psychologist Leon Festinger has shown, a commitment once made "gives rise to processes that tend to stabilize the decision."[5] After a commitment, one has to dispel the doubts that once may have existed. This tends to stimulate certainty.

In free market investing, the myriad of potentially influential factors is too numerous and changeable for anyone to master. The most insightful and judicious position may be wrong due to circumstances about which there is no awareness. The prudent investor, by accepting this as axiomatic, positions his investments to minimize the impact of unknown risks. This may be done by following the tactics outline for minimizing risk, especially by adequate diversification.

MAXIMIZING REWARDS WHILE MINIMIZING RISKS

Be aware of both risk and potential reward. You can then arrange your investments to take advantage of benefits while containing risks. Knowing that single-minded attention to either reward or risk is likely to bring poor results, the prudent investor maintains a balanced viewpoint. Success is not likely to occur to the covetous who single-mindedly pursue maximum rewards, nor to the fearful who single-mindedly attempt to fend off loss.

In a dynamic market, emotions may be stimulated that interfere with judgment. The prudent investor attempts to understand his own passions, not only for self-understanding, but also to unshackle his knowledge. An unbalanced approach is unlikely to reach its goal.

However, not everyone should have the same balance between potential benefit and risk. As befits their nature and circumstance, some people will and should place greater emphasis on safety, while others appropriately incur greater risk in order to increase the potential benefit. Investors should emphasize the one or the other according to their personal values and nature. What I am urging is that, regardless of the weight eventually given to risk or gain, every investment position be predicated upon a conjoint consideration of both.

RELATING BENEFITS TO COSTS

This strategic principle has already been implicitly introduced in the description and measures of fundamental value. Concepts of yield, P/E ratio, my C ratio, and other valuation models as well as consideration of reasonable cost all offer some service to this principle. However, the importance of relating benefits to costs deserves explicit and more complete recognition. If not observed, the losses can be disastrous.

When an investor becomes so enthralled with a particular issue or market that appropriateness of cost becomes irrelevant, he or she has climbed into the frying pan. Safety lies only in the chance that no fire is underneath; but it was probably the intensity of the flaming market that was the lure. This investor who disregards costs will buy at the top of any market, be burned, then blame not recklessness but the market. Consequently subsequent bargains will be avoided until eventually they are transformed in another mesmerizing and costly display.

Buying bargains enlarges both gains and yields. However, do not measure a bargain by its decline in price. <u>A bargain can only be identified by relating benefits to cost</u>. Bargains are often created by market overreactions where panic overrides reasonable appraisal of cost to benefit. Rumors that a company's plant in a foreign country may be expropriated may cause a drop in stock price of 20% even though the lost value is only 1%.

Festinger, who propounded the theory of cognitive dissonance alluded to above, has garnered substantial validating support. Extending the position to investing, one would expect that an investor would tend to idealize the choices he has made. Issues received from or whose purchase was advised by a particular person may take on an emotional coloring consistent with the feelings toward that person. Widely touted issues may achieve a certain "glamour." There are many avenues by which an investor may develop an emotional attraction or repulsion toward investment issues. A reversed stock that disappoints enough to crack its halo may generate antithetical feelings like an unfaithful lover. Love may turn to hate, admiration to scorn.

These extrinsic emotional attachments may invade decisions to buy, sell, retain, or avoid. Such emotions may also influence price considerations; esteemed issues may inflate toward pricelessness, scorned issues regress toward worthlessness. These are all inducements to erode reasonable cost-and-benefit relationships that the wise will resist.

Benefits relative to cost should be taken only as a strategic standard to guide one's thinking and conduct. Benefits can only be estimated, not known. Market standards change. So the appropriateness of the relationships is only a tentative estimate subject to error. Yet trying to make that estimate directs our thinking into productive channels. Ignoring it courts disaster.

Chapter 9

Tactics of Minimizing Risk

PURCHASING POWER RISK

The Problem

Fallacies

Inflation, the compounding erosion in the value of the dollar, or other currency unit, while of momentous importance to the investor is mired in falsehoods, some perpetuated by investment professionals. For example, the following statements are all false (false according to both empirical and theoretical analysis) yet are espoused by a number of investment professionals and accepted as part of the conventional wisdom: (1) gold is a hedge against inflation, (2) common stocks are not a hedge against inflation, (3) natural resources are an effective hedge against inflation. Let me repeat; these assertions are all false.

Importance

Inflation is one of the major risks, if not the major risk, confronting the investor. While varying in its intensity from time to time, over the long term, it appears almost relentless. Over the 64 years from 1933 through 1997, the value of the dollar has eroded over twelvefold (fig. 9.1). That is, an average item costing $1.00 in 1933 would have cost $12.33 in 1998. One would need more than 12 times as many dollars merely to stay even. Furthermore, this erosion did not just occur in a brief inflationary period. It proceeded persistently over 94% of the period, at an average rate of 4.5% per year.[1] Although 1984, 1985, and 1986 were hailed as disinflationary years, the continuing average rate of 3% was not so markedly distinguished, and then in June 1987, it began heading back.[2]

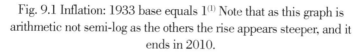

Fig. 9.1 Inflation: 1933 base equals 1[1] Note that as this graph is arithmetic not semi-log as the others the rise appears steeper, and it ends in 2010.

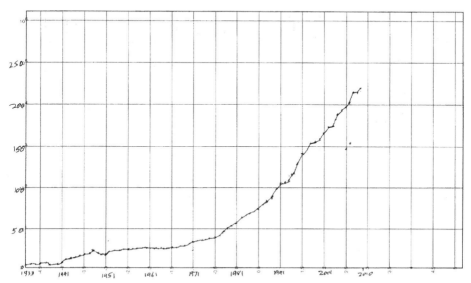

The Solution: Long-Term Emphasis on Flexible-Dollar Forms

General

Fortunately, there is a way to sidestep the insistent ravages of inflation; avoid long-term fixed-dollar forms of investment. Invest over the long term in ownership of real things, as opposed to things whose definition is anchored to units of currency. This central position should be supported by three steps. First, select for your investment those real things that may most readily adjust. Second, diversify that investment to approximate a general experience. Third, be patient. With a sharp onset of inflation, market disturbance may cause <u>short-term</u> price declines in stocks etc. Two preeminent examples of a long-term inflation hedge are common stock and real estate.

Common Stock: An Inflation Hedge

Background

Since conventional wisdom in the 1970s rejected the idea that stocks are an inflation hedge, let us take a brief look at the story of inflation and stock. Prior to about 1973, investment experts regularly regarded common stock as an inflation hedge. For example, Dowrie and Fuller, two professors of finance, writing on coping with inflation, stated, "Concentration on common stocks for this purpose . . . (is) probably the soundest course available to most investors . . ."[3] Samuelson, the noted author of economics textbooks, says, "Inflation tends to favour debtors and profit receivers at the expense of creditors and fixed-income receivers."[4] The typical stock receives profits and represents some indebtedness.

Then, following OPEC's demonstration of its power, inflation surged; and, in 1974, many companies' profits declined in response. Investors watched the stock market plummet. Some pundits looked at this and propounded the view that stocks are vulnerable to inflation.

Let me hasten to add that I agree that stocks may be vulnerable to inflation. Initially profits may be squeezed and perhaps some bankruptcies caused. Nevertheless, this must be qualified. First, if profits drop, it is likely to be only temporary. Second, if profits drop, it is likely to be a response to "cost push" inflation (company costs such as labor or materials inflate first), such as the one ignited by OPEC in 1973. Third, I would expect a later profit resurgence, the timing of which would depend upon the company's circumstances. Fourth, profits may not drop even temporarily.

Clear and Abundant Statistical Linkage

From the data for the sixty-three years from 1920 to 1983,[1] the year when inflation was reined in to more modest levels, I repeatedly found significant positive correlations between yearly fluctuations in the consumer price index and each of several indices of fundamental value of common stock. In addition, significant positive correlations between inflation and stock prices were found. *Significant* here means that the probability of the correlation occurring by chance is less than 1 out of 100 and, therefore, is taken to be intrinsic. Corporate earnings per share are the fundamental measure of corporate profits. They rise with inflation. Rates of return on invested capital are a measure of profitability. They rise with inflation. Percentages of reinvested capital to total capital are a prime measure of the basis for earnings growth. They rise with inflation. Dividends are one of the stockholder's channels of sharing in corporate profits. They rise with inflation. Revenues are the source of profits. They rise with inflation. Book values express the amounts invested into companies to form the basis for profits. They rise with inflation. All of these are indices of the increased dollar profitability caused by inflation.

All these correlations are less than perfect and therefore reflect tendencies rather than invariable relationships. Nevertheless, the statement above, "They rise with inflation," does not just mean that the two vaguely rise at the same time. The magnitude of the rise in the index of profitability tends to reflect the magnitude of the rise in inflation. Each of these correlations is significant.

Beyond these correlations, I also found that a series of significant parallel correlations existed between the consumer price index and each of the above indices averaged over the time period beginning with the year of the price rise and extending onward. Thus, inflationary rises correlate with the average profitability of the next two years, the next three years, and the next four years. These correlations indicate that although some companies may be slower to respond than others, an adjustment is made, and, after a few years, is made by almost all.

History

Putting aside the statistical links between inflation and stocks, let us turn to two historical observations. Edgar Smith, commenting in 1924 on the devastating German inflation, wrote, "What the final outcome will be cannot be foreseen, but we do know that the demoralization of currency values has completely wiped out the creditor class . . . . And the industrial leaders who, through the ownership of large blocks of common stock which control the processes of industry, and who were shrewd enough to use the depreciating Mark as a method of increasing their common stock, are to-day the most powerful men in Germany."[5]

Looking at our own recent history and using 1972 (the year before the emergent prominence of OPEC and the coincident inflationary surge) as a base, the consumer price index rose overall 265% to the end of the first quarter of 1987. Meanwhile, the S&P 500 rose 272% while paying out equally rising dividends. Those who merely sat on stocks of an average quality, thus successfully hedged that inflationary binge. The stock market in late March 1987, although high with a Value Line Composite P/E of 15.3 was actually lower than in 1972, when the P/E was 18.9. Thus, the passive stock investor did better than merely hedge, since in addition to having received dividends, his stocks were a better value than in the base period. This reflects the combination of fundamental growth added to inflationary enlargement. The boom in stocks in the 1980s may be seen as a belated recognition of the underlying real values, which had been continuously growing during the seventies.

Theory

Inflation refers to a general rise in the prices of goods and services. Since corporations, partnerships, and single proprietorships produce all of these goods and services, on average their revenues must eventually rise. Although their costs may begin rising first, companies that had been viable enterprises ought to be able eventually to compensate by revenue increases. For a company that has been profitably satisfying a societal need, there is no reason to believe that the preexisting point of intersection of demand and supply for its products would be permanently altered by a changing value of currency, except for transactions in which foreign currencies have an influence.

From a slightly different view, as the currency is debased, the prices of real things must increase. Corporate equity—along with land, oil, and lumber—is a real thing. Corporate equity reflects an enduring organizational structure of people, ideas, and resources oriented to the creation of value. This is a real value fixed not to monetary units but contingent upon its effectiveness in meeting a societal want. Corporate equity also represents ownership of knowledge, rights, and physical assets of land, buildings, and supplies. These also are things of which are not fixed to monetary units. With a debased currency, one would expect that that real value would come to command more units of currency.

Complications from Variable Impact

Although the use of variable dollar forms of investment is the theoretical hedge against inflation, it is clear that not all variable forms are equally good. Inflation does not strike the price of everything at the same time. Some goods are hit earlier and some harder than others. Thus, some variable-form investments may be at a temporary disadvantage. Indeed, some things may initially deteriorate in value in response to inflation if the inflationary impact starts with their constituent costs. A farmer who has grown a particular commodity, say watercress, may find that because inflation has raised his rent and price of fertilizer, his crop this year costs him more and that therefore the residual value, or profit, to him of his crop of watercress is less (profit = revenue - cost). Nevertheless, this decrease in value is likely to be temporary, as is suggested by a simple observation. Unless the fundamental situation of watercress has changed, the decrease in value will result in either or both: (1) a direct price increase as the farmer attempts to surmount his earnings' decrement; (2) decreasing costs by renting less land, using less fertilizer, or cutting back on paid assistance, etc. Such cost cutting would cause a corresponding decrease in production. As supply drops while demand has been unaffected, the price of watercress will tend to be supported. If the first option succeeds, nothing will have changed except for the units of currency. If the second option is tried and succeeds, profit margins will be restored, and an incentive will exist to expand again to the former point of real production.

Common stocks respond to inflation in a manner analogous to this example for watercress. Thus, some stocks may have lower earnings and consequently lower valuations in the short run, but if their customers' desire for their products or services is unchanged, price adjustments in those products or services will be made, which will restore real value.

The timing of the positive response to inflation will vary from stock to stock, commodity to commodity. The timing depends upon the ordering of inflationary pressures, the prevailing demand conditions, and the costs associated with the utilization of the service, product, commodity, or land in question. Thus, some stocks and commodities will adjust immediately, some will lag, some may decline before adjusting. Although some items may be pushed completely out of a competitive position and onto oblivion, this will only be precipitated or hastened by inflation, not ultimately caused by it. The cause will exist with the basic conditions of supply and demand facing the item.

This variability across stocks accounts for the attenuated correlations one finds between overall corporate earnings and inflation in any comparison over any particular pattern of years. Although significant, values are only around +.30 for any single year comparison. In keeping with this variable response among stocks, approximately the same size correlation will be found if one relates corporate earnings with the moving average of inflation over the two-year span beginning one year earlier. One may even average inflation over a three-year or four-year span and still find the same significant, though attenuated, relationship. The indication is that there is a clear and demonstrable relationship between corporate earnings and inflation, but that it will require a few years for the full adjustment to inflation to occur.

A number of investment advisors maintain gold to be the quintessential inflation hedge. In response to my refutation, they might say that the demand for gold is influenced by inflationary expectations. While this is true, the fact remains as stated: I found no correlation between the price of gold and inflation. If no relationship exists, it cannot effectively serve as a hedge. Perhaps then we might say that the demand for gold is partially determined not by the perception of inflation, but rather by the perception of catastrophe. Thus, it may respond to a perception of catastrophic inflation. It may even respond to merely accelerating inflation, but those who would use gold to hedge inflation will have to mix in a generous measure of fancy timing.

Let me recapitulate. To defend against inflation, flexible-dollar forms of investment held for the long term are required. The inflationary impact will be variable across such investments. Most such investments will require the patience of a long-term position before their effectiveness as hedges are validated. The best hedges will be the most reliable and quickest to respond. Speed of response will be influenced by the order of inflationary pressures, and this may be clear only in retrospect.

Desirable Accompanying Features

Inelasticity of Demand

Since most smoking is regulated by addiction to a particular level of nicotine, raising the price of cigarettes by 20% will have comparatively little impact on the number sold. Similarly, reducing the price by 20% will probably not appreciably increase sales. Its demand is said to be inelastic or relatively unresponsive to price changes. Products, services, or resources having a relatively inelastic demand will be likely to adjust to inflation rather quickly and reliably.

Simple inexpensive necessities are likely to incline toward demand inelasticity. Conversely, luxuries and easily substituted items tend to be elastic. Products having brand names that command strong customer loyalty may enjoy thereby a decreased elasticity. Stock in companies selling simple basic nonsubstitutable products or services will tend to adjust rapidly to inflation.

Competitive Position

The greater the breadth of demand for a product, service, or resource, the greater will be the ease of accommodating to inflation. The greater the control over supply, the greater will be the ease with which price increases may be passed on. Stock of a company selling inexpensive and basic consumer goods that are widely purchased and whose market position is protected (by patents, brand-name loyalty, lowest production cost, etc.) will be in a good position to adjust to inflation. A drug company may be a good example.

The ability of a commodity to adjust to inflation is likely to be strongly related to the competitive position of its suppliers. Unless a commodity is protected by a favorable supply position, it will probably be a poor hedge because its vulnerability to price increases.

Diversification

While in the long run land in general may be reliably counted on to adjust to inflation, the same may not be quite so true for the particular parcel of land that we may hold. Its particularity may be such as to impair the breadth of demand for the property, and hence its ability to adjust its price. Consider, for example, a plot of residential land situated next to a recently defunct sugar mill in a remote rural setting with no other viable economic base.

Narrowness of product line enlarges the unpredictability as a hedge. Indeed, part of the attenuation of the correlation between common stocks and inflation is attributable to the inclusion in common stocks of companies dominated by one or two commodities. Timber companies and copper mining are two examples of such commodity-dominated industries that have had difficulties in coping with inflation. For example, in the period 1968 to 1983, the consumer price index increased by 288% while the earnings of a sample of seven forest product companies grew only half as much and while a sample of seven copper companies suffered an earnings decrease of 84%. It should be noted that these examples involve ownership of basic resources, which many advisors have touted as an inflation hedge.

Because its generality imparts greater reliability, a portfolio of stocks in different industries, each representing multiple products or services, is likely to be one of the best ships to safely traverse the unsettled seas of inflation. This is especially so if the stocks represent growing companies with relatively inelastic products sold from a favorable competitive position.

The view that common stock is the premier hedge is contrary to the generally accepted conception. Therefore, ironically, in a time of dramatically increasing inflation, which galvanizes attention to the problem of inflation, stocks will probably face a sell-off as investors try to find shelter in gold or natural resources. From a long-term point of view, this is no problem because the fundamental underlying value is most likely to be growing. It will only be a question of time before stock prices catch up with the underlying value. In the meantime, the astute investor may find himself faced with a dazzling display of bargains in the stock market. This was of course the position of those purchasing stocks in the late 1970s as inflation was rolling onward, with corporate earnings and dividends reaching new heights while stock prices dwindled. Such investors may have subsequently experienced better than a tripling of the prices of their stocks and still not found them overpriced. The stock market boom of the early and mid-eighties was a belated recognition of the enhanced dollar values in common stocks caused largely by the preceding inflation.

Growing Value

Among the flexible-dollar investment media, some exhibit persistent growth totally aside from and in addition to mere inflationary adjustment. The long-term increase in value from growth may assist the upward adjustment to inflation and, if not, will at least provide movement in the right direction.

Common stocks may be expected to grow because of their periodic reinvestment of profits as well as the swelling population of customers. Land value in general and over the long term may be expected to grow because while the supply is basically fixed, the demand must relentlessly grow with population pressure. We may also expect increase in the value of a resource whose supply is being exhausted and for which there is no readily available equally inexpensive substitute. Oil prices might fall due to temporary oversupply. Yet unless major new supplies are found, eventually prices will have to resume their escalation until they reach the level of the next most inexpensive fuel option, possibly either alcohol or shale oil.

Very few other things will follow the growth patterns indicated above. Even natural resources having a finite supply are likely to have their availability so far in the future that no limiting response on supply will be felt for decades or centuries. While more people may use more gold, silver, or diamonds, clearly they also may not. While land has a clear utilitarian underpinning to its value, these items do not. Although gold, silver, and diamonds have utilitarian functions, their prices have encouraged substitutes to replace them. Their market demand is now largely formed by cultural conventions regarding status. These of course are arbitrary and not at all immutable.

NONSYSTEMATIC MARKET RISK

You can best minimize nonsystematic market risk by observing a few procedures. If one follows the following six tactics, nonsystematic market risk will in all probability be contained well within acceptable limits.

Diversification

The prudent investor who regards him—or herself as fallible recognizes that even the positions taken with the greatest confidence may go bad. Our investments are subject to possible surprising dramatic shifts in fortune from sources outside of our awareness. Unexpected developments may be positive or negative, crucial or inconsequential. Adequate diversification provides an essential defense against the sudden intrusion of nonsystematic misfortunes or disasters.

The fundamental idea of diversification is to spread the nonsystematic sources of risk. In a large-enough sample of issues, unforeseen misfortunes are likely to be offset in whole or in part by unanticipated strokes of good fortune. Beyond this, one has limited the risk of loss from any one unknown nonsystematic source.

If you hold a portfolio of twenty evenly represented stocks, and then in a sudden surprising revelation, one is dramatically soured, you can lose no more than 5% of your portfolio. If you are reasonably current in reviewing your holdings, you may limit this significantly. Even if you take a 25% beating on that issue, your overall loss is only somewhat more than 1%. Moreover, in a large-enough sample, there is only one reason to believe that fortunate events are less likely to occur than infelicitous ones. That one exception is that, having exclusively selected companies with favorable situations, one thereby may have slightly increased the possibility of future negative development, as in a regression to the mean. Nevertheless, there is a distinct possibility that, in this example, some unexpected good fortune will have occurred in the other nineteen stocks. In a large-enough sample, partially counterbalancing strokes of fortune may occur. Of course, this not only cushions against adversity, but also blunts good fortune.

Diversification does not mean a mindless inclusion of a variety of industries in a portfolio. For instance, there is no merit to buying an airline issue merely to round out one's portfolio. Including a representative sample of industries is not the point of diversification. Adequate diversification requires limiting a particular potential source of risk to an acceptable degree.

Since one obvious source of risk is from within a company, it is prudent to limit the representation in any company. Studies have suggested that an even dispersion over from fifteen to twenty-five companies is optimal. More than this provides little benefit from decreasing risk while eroding the benefits of selective judgment.

Industrial groupings usually represent common areas of risk, so diversification should accordingly be made across industries. The purchase of fifteen different banking issues, while protecting against company-specific risk, would leave one extremely vulnerable to a few specific unfavorable developments touching the banking industry as a whole.

One should look to commodity of risk and not be blinded by industrial names. Gannett, Dun & Bradstreet, and RR Donnelley frequently have been grouped together as publishers; but, while they have the common business of providing information, the differences in type of information they provide are significant. Customers to whom they sell and means of reaching the customer are so different as to reflect virtually no commonality of industrial risk.

Avoidance of Unmarketable Issues

Some stocks, partnership interests, and other forms of investment have very poor marketability. This may arise from specific restrictions regarding transfers, extremely large valuations of each share, or simply from a limitation in potentially interested purchasers. While such investments may perform well, they may be exceedingly difficult to sell if their fortunes reverse, or even if one merely requires the use of the invested sum for another purpose. At such times, a sale may be possible only by accepting a substantial discount from basic value.

A substantial problem with marketability is most likely to arise from investments in partnerships, small unlisted family corporations, and new companies having hope as the major credential. Although such companies may have great merit, they do pose a greater-than-usual risk of loss arising from the difficulty in selling for full value.

DIRECT FINANCIAL RISK

Whether financial risk affects you directly or through the market, some of the tactics by which to protect yourself will be the same: (1) select according to financial strength and then (2) diversify. In addition, because of the unique importance of this risk, insurance is often available. Federal insurance on bank and savings and loan association saving accounts has protected more than a few investors. Brokerage firms may have insurance to protect customers' securities on deposit with them. Yet the mere fact of insurance should not lull you to doze in complacency. If the insurer is faced with many simultaneous claims, funds could be insufficient. Do not forget your primary protections against direct financial risk: financial strength and diversification.

As with other kinds of risk, the assumption of the risk may or may not provide a benefit. The interest paid on an uninsured account in a financially weak finance company is likely to be high. In return for the somewhat-increased risk from placing your portfolio of securities in the street name of a brokerage firm, you derive a certain convenience.

SYSTEMATIC MARKET RISK

Maintain Enough Cash Equivalent Reserves

Adequate cash or equivalent reserves provide two indispensable advantages. First, they protect you against being forced to sell at a bad time. Second, they let you take advantage of investment opportunities as they occur. Major losses will occur if one sells after prices have plummeted following a market crash, especially if one had purchased them at the previous high. Nevertheless, if you have been following a long-term fundamental value-oriented approach, one need not be daunted by even a steep decline in the prices of your investments. A cyclical bottom is characterized by an abundance of bargains and is a time not to sell, but to buy if the value is there. A minimum defensive tactic is to continue holding one's long-term position. If one avoids a sale, no loss will be realized.

Reserves may be invested in positions that may be liquidated at any time with no loss. The holding of treasury bills, other short-term interest-bearing notes, or money market funds that permit immediate withdrawal are all appropriate ways to keep one's reserve. The usefulness of a reserve depends on both, the rapidity with which money may be withdrawn and the minimization of risk of loss for quick withdrawal. The shortness of time to maturity is a protection against adverse market swings. If the price of treasury bills falls, at worst you only have to wait for the remainder of the ninety-day life of the bill to retrieve all of your money without loss. In addition, because it is redeemable at par in ninety or fewer days, its price cannot drop far. Thus, even if you have to sell before maturity, you will likely be very close to a breakeven.

Shifting Emphasis across Markets

Obviously one of the ways to protect oneself from a systematic drop in the market is to get one's investments out of the market beforehand. According to this strategy, before a serious drop in the stock market, one would sell one's stock and buy instead something that is not vulnerable to the same market risk. The alternate investment might simply be short-term cash equivalents, or one could invest in other markets such as bonds, real estate, or commodities if one perceived them largely immune from the same influence believed to pose a threat to the stock market. One can also shift between different subsections of a major market. That is, one could shift from one type of stock to another type of stock that reacts differently, or a Swiss bond instead of an American bond.

You can also nullify your exposure to systematic market risk while maintaining your portfolio of stock in place. This can be done by hedging with a short sale of stock index futures. The efficiency of this method depends upon the correspondence between your portfolio and the stock index future selected and upon the dollar equivalence between the portfolio held and the futures sold. Nevertheless, because of (1) the accumulated cost of extended hedging and (2) the eradication of your potential for stock value increase, this is not recommended for anything longer than a short-term adjustment. Since short-term movements are not very predictable, it is not generally recommended for such use either.

Gradual Shift in Emphasis

As with other simplistic notions, one should temper the above strategy before extracting its little kernel of merit. Mindful that we are subject to error, prudence dictates rejecting a categorical all-or-none approach and instead gradually shifting the degree of market representation.

Being entirely out of the portfolio may pose just as great a risk as being in at the wrong time. Indeed, if one is concerned with the stock market and has a long-term viewpoint, it is more risky to be out of the market than in it. Although timing is crucial for executing short-term movements, the prediction of such movements is fraught with difficulty. An example is provided by one preeminent market guru with supposed mastery of market timing who advocated abandoning the stock market just days before it was to skyrocket on the first leg of a bull market, which five years later was still in progress. As the stock market is the long-term beneficiary of both accumulated growth and inflation, one's long-term priority ought to be to remain in the stock market. Transfer out of the stock market should be made with care.

Shift in Response to Distinct Signs of Risk

Movement out of the stock market should not only be gradual; but also, each step should be taken only in response to a specific indication of increased market risk. One's perspective should not be on the pattern of market action or the prediction of the time of onset of a bear market. Market prediction is hazardous. Instead, respond to distinct signs of increasing risk, such as the following:

Overpricing

When the various indices of value reveal that the prices of one's stocks and those of the market generally are overpriced, one should be alert to the concomitant risk. Specifically, look at P/E ratios, yields, C ratios, as well as estimates of absolute value (derived both by discounted future receipts and by current interest rate or inflation-related methods). These should be looked at from the perspective of historical standards, while nevertheless being aware that historical standards are subject to change. When current prices are around or below long-term market averages, no sign of risk from this direction is revealed and the degree of market representation in stocks may be maintained at normal levels (at perhaps from 90% to 95%, depending upon one's reserve requirements and comfortable and knowledgeable access to other markets having a flexible-dollar form, such as real estate. This estimate leaves aside an investment in one's home). Be aware that the conventionally recommended proportion of stock is markedly lower and, I believe, misinformed.

The average P/E of the Dow Jones stocks over the period 1920 to 1983 was 13.59. The average P/E of the Value Line Composite 900 industrial, retail, and transportation companies over the period 1962-84 was 14.17. The average P/E for the S&P 500 for this later period was 13.15. Both the average and the variability of index P/Es vary slightly across indices, with the Dow Jones being the least extreme (in both average and variability), the S&P intermediate, and Value Line Composite the most extreme of these three. In spite of these small differences, we may say that when a broad stock market average P/E is at 14 or less, there is no cause to worry from this quarter.

As the broad market average P/E rises past 18, we are at about one standard deviation (σ) above the mean. Assuming that the distribution of market average indices is normal, this is a level where 84% of the time the market is lower and 16% of the time it is higher. This point is high enough to justify some movement out of the market, if one's particular stocks and tax situation warrant. A drop of commitment in stocks to perhaps 80% of one's portfolio or less is not out of order. If other value indicators indicate similar extremity, the suggestion to decrease exposure to stocks should be taken, unless clearly contradicted by other economic considerations.

As the market average P/E rises to around 22, prices are about two standard deviations (σ) above the mean. Only about 2% of the time are prices this high. Consequently the risk is appreciable. At this level, reduction in the holding of stock to 50% of one's total investments or less is appropriate, providing (1) other indices of value are equally extreme, (2) the tax consequences are not ruinous, and (3) the nature of the stock market, and hence its averages, have not undergone a substantial change.

Two cautions are in order. First, do not be lulled into thinking that a 20% capital gains tax is insignificant. When combined with a state tax and the alternate minimum tax, the sale of an issue you have held for long time could lose over 40% of its value. Even sustaining a 50% drop in market price might be preferable. Of course, in an IRA or similar tax-exempt account, this consideration is not relevant. Second, although many investors have taken big losses by convincing themselves that the market had so significantly changed that historical benchmarks were inapplicable, it is indeed possible that such a change might occur.

At an <u>average index</u> P/E of 26, prices have reached the third standard deviation (σ) above the mean where they are close to the 99.9[th] percentile. Just slightly more than one in one thousand times will prices be expected to equal or exceed these levels, if historical standards continue to prevail and the distribution is normal. This suggests extraordinary risk and, if the P/Es of one's own holding are comparable, warrants drastically drawing down the holding of stock to 20% or even lower if decent opportunities exist in other markets, such as real estate, and even gold—in spite of what I have said about it—since it would be a temporary dodge.

The four points I have mentioned above (the mean and the first, second, and third standard deviations above the mean) I intend only as benchmark examples. As investors, we will face a continuum of extremity of prices and attendant risks to which to accommodate. As values begin to be significantly overpriced, begin to move out of stocks, if appropriate. As the levels of extremity mount, increase the rapidity of movement away from stocks. Rough guides to judge the extremity of expensiveness from the C ratio and yield are presented in table 9.1.

<u>Yet bear in mind, movement out of the market should never be made only on the basis of such benchmark figures</u>. One must always consider such other factors as the following: the quality, extremity of price, and possible future of one's particular stocks, the tax impact, and the situation in alternative

markets. Use these benchmark figures only in reference to the broad market averages.

Table 9.1 Benchmark figures for C Ratio
and Yield extracted from the Value Line
Composite 900 Index[6]

Position	C Ratio	Yield
Mean	1.18	3.53
1σ above Mean	1.64	2.74
2σ above Mean	2.10	1.96
3σ above Mean	2.56	1.18

No equivalent benchmark figures exist for the measures of absolute value. Nevertheless, when current prices are clearly above calculations, retention of the stock is called into question. Bear in mind the guiding principle for investment sales. Sell only if the funds diminished by transaction costs and taxes would be more productive than the present amount in its present form.

Emerging Prospects of a Depression

Depression or significant recession not only means hard times for employees in jeopardy for their jobs, but also for owners as profits and dividends stagnate or fall. As prospects for a depression emerge, systematic market risk increases. One possible response to this increased risk is to decrease stock market representation. Still this is only one possible response to be judged in light of the situation as it exists. Since the market is a leading indicator, by the time the prospects of a depression have become clear, the market may already have finished its downward correction.

Most of us will have to rely upon economic experts to advise us when a depression is approaching. Of course, they will do so in abundance if we listen to their public statements, but they may not be in agreement. It may help us to at least have a crude conception of what a depression is. Therefore, let us consider a depression to be the result of an insufficiency of demand for goods and services relative to the supply. When such an insufficiency accumulates, the eventual response must be a shutting down of supply, that is, production or provision, until equilibrium is reestablished. One nasty difficulty, however, is that shutting down production may also pull down demand, as income from work falls. This would be indeed a vicious cycle, and without new inputs, a drop of severe proportions is possible. Such things as primarily tax reductions but also unemployment insurance, welfare, and governmentally induced demand through deficit spending may for a time diminish the likelihood and potency of such a vicious cycle.

This low demand does not usually result from a lack of desire, as it does in cases over production where one doesn't want more than a sufficient number of the product. Rather, it comes from an inability to effectively express that desire. (People wanting to consume may refrain because they do not have the money.) Thus, a more important solution may come from an increase in money supply such as by tax cuts that allow a resurgence of investment and jobs to turn the depression around.

Footsteps signaling the approach of a depression include widespread excessive supply and failing demand. Signs of excessive supply could be large and rising inventories or productive and service overcapacity. A plant making less than half the widgets it could make reveals its productive overcapacity. When restaurants with idle waiters fill less than half of their tables, a service overcapacity exists. These are signs of excessive supply relative to demand and warn of impending adjustment. The severity of the adjustment will depend upon the severity of the excess and what steps are taken for correction.

From the other direction, demand could be blocked by restrictive financial or monetary situations, like excessive interest rates, draining taxes, or overvaluation of the dollar relative to other currencies. A sharp rise in consumer debt could limit future demand, first by imposing a greater debt-servicing requirement; second, by constraining further debt-financed consumption; and third by a possible satiation of desire for consumption in the near future. Domestic demand could also be hampered by superior foreign products and by domestic wages and prices adamantly resistant to downward adjustments.

More direct measures of recession, such as falling industrial production or gross national product, may be by themselves less helpful predictors for a couple of reasons. First, a small brief fall in production may be an appropriately adjustive economic response leading to a restoration of equilibrium. Second, by the time such a fall has occurred, the stock market is likely to have reacted also.

While attention to such signs may allow one to limit possible losses, a gradual and measured response to danger remains appropriate. Since the long-term movement of the stock market has been upward for as long as statistics have been gathered and since there is every reason to believe this will continue, a long-term position chosen with care and accompanied by adequate reserves may do well even if unsold before a depression or other market reversal. Sufficient time has given full recovery from every depression, including the Great Depression. In contrast, some upward movements once missed have proven unrecoverable.

Attention to Defensive Criteria in Selection

Stocks vary in their vulnerability to systematic risk. They vary in their vulnerability to depression. <u>One possible response to gathering signs of market reversal is to switch from more—to less-vulnerable stocks</u>. As an alternative to movement away from stocks, one can change from one kind of stock to another. While this will not remove systematic risk, it can attenuate it. A combination of the two responses may be the most effective.

Specific Defensive Selection Criteria

A few specific criteria may help select those stocks that are more resistant to systematic risk, including the risk from depression. You can use these for selecting all stocks, or just when systematic danger signals are strong, according to your desire for protection from this source.

Low-Beta Index

The beta index is a measure of the volatility of a stock's price relative to the market as a whole. A stock having a beta of 1.00 has volatility equal to the weighted average of all stocks on the New York Stock Exchange and will tend to move proportionately with the market. Stocks with a higher beta, say 1.50, will have much more pronounced movements. A stock with a low beta, say 0.6, will have mild price fluctuations. Stocks with low betas, therefore, present less risk of adverse systematic market influences.

Resistance to Cyclical Influences

Some sectors of the economy are very responsive to cyclical business factors. Activity in these industries alternately surges and recedes. While in many cases the stimuli propelling the alternations are limited in scope and specific in their influence to only a few industries, most influences have a widespread impact. These are the conditions that lead toward or away from recessions and depressions.

Industries and companies vary in their strength of response to these conditions. "Cyclical companies" respond strongly with fluctuations between boom and slack. "Defensive companies" are at the other extreme, having minimal and delayed response to general business conditions. The stock of such defensive companies tends to fare better against depressions and other adverse systematic movements. While cyclical companies are experiencing P/E ratio shrinkage multiplied by underlying earning shrinkage, defensive stocks may simply be experiencing P/E ratio shrinkage, which furthermore may be comparatively modest because of their less negative outlook.

The most cyclical and least defensive companies are the manufacturers of expensive capital equipment; those who supply the equipment to other companies. The most defensive are those selling highly desired and inexpensive services or goods for immediate consumption, providing that there are no cheaper substitutes. Toothpaste, tobacco, telephone, basic medical supplies, and nonspecialty food processing are good examples of defensive companies. Note that while tobacco stocks are prey to significant specific risk due to anti-tobacco influences, they are relatively protected from systematic risk.

General Selection Criteria Applicable to Market Risk

Among those criteria for stock selection presented earlier for protection against nonsystematic market risk, a few also offer some protection against systematic market risk. Some of these provide even greater protection than the criteria specifically designed for this purpose mentioned above. Notable are the following:

Reasonable Price

If a reasonable price has been paid for the stock, it will have less room to fall much below costs. Reasonably priced stock could not have been purchased at a speculatively frenzied market top.

Financial Strength

A financially strong company will be better able to cope with negative systematic business influences. Its resources may enable it to weather a depression that would force another company under.

Avoidance of Glamour

This criterion is—strictly speaking—unnecessary since having observed the standard of reasonable price, you will not have bought a glamour issue. Still, it is worth mentioning because the purchasers of glamour stocks are the people most at risk in an adverse systematic market reaction.

INVESTOR EXPANSION OF MARKET RISK

Not all investors are aware that some ways of investing increase risk. Avoid increasing your risk unless you decide the increase is warranted by the reasonable prospect of greater benefits. The astute and wary investor may do the following:

Avoid Time Constraint

Chapter 6 on risk indicated that placing constraints on the period of time an investment is held greatly increases risk. You can avoid such investor-created risk enlargement by avoiding time-bound investments. This means avoiding options and warrants as primary investment media. It also means avoiding short sales. Although, when used as hedges against opposing risks, these instruments and tactics are appropriate.

Avoid Impairing Flexibility

There remains another group of time-bound investments that may seem quite innocuous, but nevertheless contain a related risk. These are fixed-term deposits like CDs, savings and loan and bank money market accounts, and other time-constrained deposits. When you know you do not want to use the funds until after the fixed time period ends, their use is quite appropriate. Also, if such funds are used as a primary investment in their own right, they do not significantly enhance risk. You can reduce risk by having a number of time-bound investments with staggered ending dates.

Still, when such funds are used as a cash reserve, they do carry added risk. The terminal date of such accounts is unhappily unlikely to exactly coincide with the moment you want to use it. One would thus either forgo the investment opportunity or step into a penalty.

Be Aware of the Relationship between Risk and Time to Maturity

Increasing the length to maturity of a bond increases the risk to principal, although this risk from time to time may be warranted by the corresponding decrease in risk to income as well as by the potential for increased gains. Since the general odds are not against the investor on this (as they are with short sales, margin purchases, and so forth), one should feel quite free to assume this added risk when it appears warranted.

Chapter 10

Optimizing Benefits

The expert can gather the benefits that his or her special expertise may permit. The knowledgeable toiler may lavish the time necessary to attempt to extract extra benefit from the several markets' cyclical vicissitudes. The gambler whose motto is "multimillionaire or broke" will plunge into risk, using leverage and time-bound mechanisms as the springboard to propel him into the depths of his hunches. The wealthy may retain experts with discretionary power.

Yet what about the intelligent layman of no great wealth to invest ($2,000 to $5,000,000) who does not wish to spend a lot of time, but who wants to protect and expand his or her savings and build a second income? How do such people get the most from their investment? How can you do this while preserving both your investment and peace of mind?

RIDE THE LONG-TERM EXPANSIONARY FORCE IN STOCKS

Fortunately, one of the more robust market forces is also the most predictable. This combination makes it inviting to the patient investor as an avenue to acceptable rewards with simultaneously reduced risk and bother. This is the long-term expansionary force in stocks.

The Expansionary Force

Scanning a chart of the Dow Jones Industrial Index across a broad stretch of time, two salient features immediately leap to awareness. First, it is relentlessly fluctuating. Second, the fluctuations trend very clearly upward. This second feature illustrates the tendency of common stocks to increase in price. Figure 10.1 is a semilogarithmic chart of the yearly range of the Dow Jones Industrial Average.[1] Such a chart has the virtue of showing equal percentages as equal distances; thus, the distance between 1 and 10 is the same as between 100 and 1,000. Nevertheless, it does severely blunt the appearance of growth and fluctuation.

Figure 10.2 shows the underlying impetus for this uptrend in prices: the continuing upward movement of the average per share earnings, dividends, and book value of the index stocks. (1) Earnings in 1932 were negative and, as the chart is semilogarithmic, are omitted. The increasing trend of the Dow has been persistent. In spite of the fluctuating pattern, in 62% of the years from 1920 through 1994, earnings increased over the prior year; in 73%, dividends increased; and in 82%, book value grew. During that seventy-five-year span, the longest stretch of time without an earnings increase was four years during the Great Depression.

Fig. 10.1 DJIA Yearly Price Ranges[1]

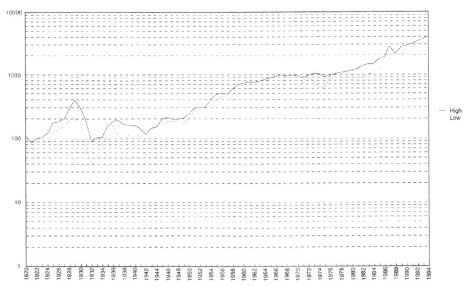

The expansionary strength is substantial. From a 1921 average of about 75 to a 1987 level of 2,500 is a thirty-three-fold increase in spite of the intervention of the Great Depression. This reflects an average compound price increase of 5.4% per year. From 1987 to 1998, the average yearly compound price increase was 9%. From 1920 to 1983, average earnings increased at an average compound rate of 5.2% per year.[2] When added to the 4.7% average yield across that period, the average benefit to the investor was 9.9% per year. This is not bad when one considers that it reflects a market average. With decent selectivity, one might well have improved upon this substantially.

Fig. 10.1 DJIA Earnings, Dividends, and Book Value[1]

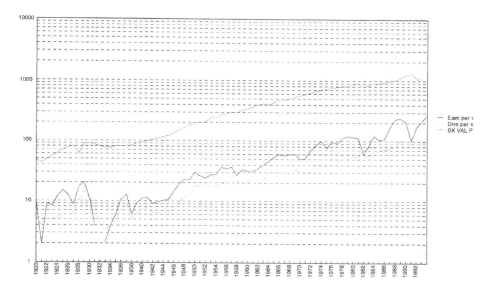

Other stock market indices affirm this picture of fluctuations superimposed on a dominant uptrend. The Value Line Industrial Composite, which reflects the average experience of 900 industrial, retail, and transportation companies, is a broader index of the market than the Dow Jones. With these less-mature companies, the upward trend is even more pronounced. Over the most recent twenty-four years for which I have immediately available data (1961-1985), stock prices rose at an annually compounding rate of 5.8%. Meanwhile, earnings rose at a compound rate of 8.2% per year and dividends at 6.2% per year, for an average yearly total benefit of 14.4%.[3]&[4] The relationship between progression of time and progression of earnings is robust and reliable as indicated by a correlation coefficient of +.94 (p < .01). This is impressively high and indicates a strong bond: 88% ($.94^2$) of the variation in yearly earnings is bound up with the progression of time. The + indicates that they move in the same direction; as the years advance so do earnings.

The Dual Engines of Increase

This increasing trend in earnings and consequently also in dividends, book value, and market price is powered by two forces described earlier:

inflation and <u>fundamental growth</u>. As we have seen, stocks make continuing, though at times belated, adjustments to inflation. The pundits will tell you that a sudden upsurge in inflation will cause stocks to fall; they do not tell you that as stocks adjust, the long-term effect is to increase stock prices. Revenues, percent earned on capital, earnings, reinvested capital, and dividends—each make compensating adjustments. Indeed, percent earned on total capital surges in response to accelerating inflation. Excepting only stocks of moribund companies, stock prices cannot lag too far behind such expansion of underlying valuation.

For the twenty-two years surrounding the propounding of the modish dictum that stocks do not hedge inflation, 1962 to 1984,[3]&[4] the correlation between earnings, changes of the Value Line Industrial Composite, and yearly changes in the consumer price index was +.68 (p < .01). The suggestion is that perhaps about 47% of the increase in earnings was related to inflation.

In addition to this adjustment process, continual new real investments are being financed by retained earnings. These form the basis for <u>real growth</u> (beyond merely monetary increase). This persistent impetus toward growth, added to the upward adjustment to inflation (in an era of built-in tendencies toward inflation), results in the clear expansionary tendency for common stocks.

It may seem inappropriate to view adjustments to inflation as a benefit. Indeed, I subscribe to this view myself. I prefer to think of adjustments to inflation as illusory benefits. The ability of stocks to compensate for the ravages of inflation is more accurately seen as a defense against risk than as a benefit. I wish to emphasize that gains made as an adjustment to inflation are really illusory. If I can take my dollar-doubled investment and only buy the same things as I could have previously, I have gained no new thing. My "benefit" is that I have avoided a loss.

Yet we must make comparative judgments vis-à-vis other investment alternatives. For all of these other investment alternatives, dollar values customarily are taken at constant face value. For an instrument like a bond that is absolutely unprotected from inflation, we make no subtraction for the loss. Only in this sense, for the purpose of making comparative judgments, do I speak of the avoidance of an inflationary loss as a "benefit." It does represent value actually received, only value saved.

Two Forms of Benefits

There are two distinct forms of benefits to be obtained from this expansionary force. You may choose to seek one or the other or a blend of the two. The latter will probably be suggested by circumstances. These alternative objectives are the following:

Growing Dividend Stream

The increasing value of the expansionary force can be used to supply an expanding stream of dividends. Over the long term, the growth of dividends generally will be limited by the growth in earnings, although in the short term, dividends may continue to grow while earnings are temporarily stunted.

Following this tactic of holding stocks for long-term dividend growth can result in impressive eventual yields on the original value invested. With an average growth in earnings of only 5.2%, after ten years, a sum originally invested at a yield of 4.7% may yield 7.8% on the original sum. After twenty years, this may grow to 12.95%, after thirty years 21.5%, and after forty years over 35.7% <u>per year</u>. Such an increase would reflect the <u>average historical</u> growth shown over the past sixty-three years, <u>without any reinvestment of dividends by the investor</u>. It's possible to do better.

What could you expect if you matched only the modest average historical growth of the mature Dow Jones stocks? If at age thirty, you invested $10,000 at 5% and added $1,200 at 5% each year for the following forty years, at age seventy, you would receive over $10,750 per year in dividends from over $215,000 of principal, after having received more than $168,000 in dividends, enough to have paid for your $1,200 yearly addition and allowed you over $121,000 to have spent on added consumption. This, of course, assumes that (1) the average growth rate continues to prevail and (2) at age seventy we are on trend line. I do not advance these figures seriously except as an illustration of what average experience is capable of providing across time.

The investor who wants to follow this tactic of income building should be able to improve upon this blind average experience. For instance, had you bought Merck in 1982, after sixteen years, your yield would have reached 48.6% of your cost. There are three tools at your disposal for the attempt at improvement. First is <u>selection</u>. One may select according to rapidity and predictability of dividend growth. Second is <u>modification</u>. The investor may monitor the portfolio to make changes as warranted by changing circumstances.

Third is <u>reinvestment</u>. One may reinvest a portion of dividends. This will tend to increase the average rate of growth by a percentage approximately the same as the percentage reinvested.

Capital Gains

One may alternatively invest with an eye toward increasing the total sum of money or principal invested. In following this tactic, one may choose to invest in companies that are reinvesting a larger portion of earnings rather than paying them out in dividends. This accomplishes the same result as reinvesting one's dividends, except that if the company simply retains them for direct reinvestment, there is a saving on taxes and commissions.

In choosing between gains versus a rising income stream, there are opposed considerations. Taxes are likely to be changed. If capital gains may be taxed at a different rate than dividends. In making your choice, consider the tax consequences of each. Note that leaving the stock in place and taking its growing dividends avoids the extra tax on capital accumulation and cost of commissions.

<u>Requirements</u>

The long-term expansionary force cannot be used successfully without adhering to the basic orientation introduced in the chapter on strategy. An orientation toward <u>fundamental value</u> is required. Likewise, a <u>long-term perspective</u> must be maintained. Without these, you may embark on the investment seas; but, without a course and compass, you will be tossed here and there. Failure to use a <u>multivariate approach</u> is like concentrating on the rudder, without awareness of the set of the sails. Failure to <u>accept fallibility</u> is like sailing without a lifeboat. Failure to <u>relate benefits to costs</u> is like sailing on the tack that maximizes favorable winds with complete disregard for one's destination. Failure to keep an <u>adequate cash equivalent reserve</u> is like having inadequate supplies to see you through the doldrums.

The investor will be inundated with contrary patterns of thought and advice. Newspapers, magazines, circulars, television shows, brokers, and friends will tout stocks set to perform well and describe and predict short-term market action. Acquaintances will brag of quick profits, while omitting mention of reverses—until they seek financial help. Some of these views may contain interesting and even helpful information, but you should be aware of discrepant assumptions. If you shift your assumptions, let it be from your specific decision that it is appropriate to do so, not from a silent erosion that occurs outside of awareness.

Tactics of Using the Long-Term Uptrend

Selection Criteria

Growth Rate

You may wish to enhance growth by selecting stocks according to rate of growth. Since earnings are fundamental to growth, the key growth index to inspect is earnings growth. This is true regardless of whether one is interested in growth in dividends or stock price. Though if one is interested in increasing dividends, one ought to look secondarily at dividend growth to glean the likely dividend policy.

Some people look to price growth in the short term as an indicator of "momentum" (a term which assumes that market price movements have quantifiable inertia). Following "momentum"—like riding on a tiger's back—requires agility, concentration, and most of all, luck. You are unlikely to know what's there until sometime after the fact, and it's a short-term phenomenon, which can end abruptly, sometimes with a biting reversal. However, price growth in any form is not a fundamental long-term index to use. High growth rates in the price of stock are likely to mean that it is no longer the bargain it may once have been. High rates of price growth are not auspicious unless accompanied by equivalent or higher rates of earnings growth.

With respect to rate of earnings growth, you may find it preferable to eschew the spectacular highest growth rates for the more modest but still robust rates. There are two reasons for this. First, spectacular rates of 50% per year or higher are unlikely to be long continued. They usually reflect initial entry into a market. Later, market saturation and the attraction of competitors are likely to squeeze growth rates. Second, spectacular growth rates are likely to be accompanied by equally spectacular P/E ratios. Should spectacular growth slow to merely superb, these will also fall and accentuate price declines.

From 1974 through 1982, stocks with annual growth rates around 20% or higher could be found, which would also meet the other criteria for growth: suitable predictability and cost. At that time, and undoubtedly again when stocks are in less favor, such a portfolio could be assembled with stocks ranging in estimated growth rates from a low of 12%, a high of 22%, and a mean of 15%. If such an average estimated growth rate actually did prevail, and many have in the past, one would see a fourfold increase in a decade and an eightfold increase in fifteen years.

Predictability of Growth

Some companies have very predictable earnings growth. They may have recorded earnings growth over every one of the past sixteen years, with a range of growth each year ranging from a low 7% to a high of 16%. If, in addition to such historical consistency, consideration of the company's current and probable future situation reveals no reason to believe change is likely, considerable confidence may be placed in the estimate for earning growth over the next few years.

On the other hand, some companies' growth rates are only predictable precariously if at all. A company may have a good overall average growth over the past sixteen years, but show an erratic pattern. Such a company may have eight years of earnings gains and eight of losses over the past sixteen, ranging from a 15% decrease to 50% increase. Consideration of its business may show that it is at the mercy of certain unstable commodity prices. With such a company, the layperson would have extremely limited confidence in predicting growth.

A high growth rate that cannot be predicted with confidence is worth very little. If one is concerned with magnitude of future growth, one must also, and to the same degree, be concerned with the predictability of that growth.

Good Price

If an amount has been paid for a stock that cannot be justified by its current earnings and future prospects, then one may have little future price or dividend growth to anticipate. No investment purpose can be confidently expected when this standard is violated.

Periodic Review

Unless we have entered the market close to some critical juncture, it is likely that some of the stocks we have selected will do better than expected and some worse. For some, the change may be merely temporary, while for others an adjustment of long-term prospects may be due. Among stocks in which we did not invest, some bargains may have developed.

Because of these changing circumstances, a periodic review of one's portfolio and look at investment opportunities is appropriate. A review should be made at least once every half year, although every quarter is better. A deteriorated situation may be brought to your attention sooner and, of course, should be studied at that time. If a stock's situation appears fundamentally deteriorated, and despite the tax impact its retention no longer seems justified against the background of investment alternatives, it should be sold and the proceeds put to better use.

One difficulty is to discriminate between a temporary situation and a fundamental long-term change. One can attempt to identify the cause of the problem (with the aid of the investment advisory services available) and ascertain whether this can be surmounted in the future. If in doubt, you may choose to continue retention for a while to allow the picture to clarify, unless an immediate sale looks particularly attractive, for example, due to current high price. If you are somewhat more pessimistic, but still in doubt, you may equivocate by selling a portion now and allowing the remainder more time.

Do not sell a stock because it has doubled, trebled, or even quintupled in price. Sell it only when your planned use of the funds, after being shrunk from transaction costs and taxes, is preferable to retention of your present holding with its undiminished value. A sharp price increase may indeed be an appropriate trigger for a sale, but only if it has resulted in the issue being extensively overpriced.

However, one wants to preserve appropriate diversification. One stock may have appreciated so that it dominates the portfolio. If it contains half the portfolio value, then a partial sale is indicated if other opportunities are attractive.

MAINTAIN A FLEXIBLE RESERVE

The use of a cash equivalent reserve has already been described as a risk control device. This is its most important function. For this alone, it deserves mention under optimizing benefits because it permits the long-term stock positions to remain in place. Without such a reserve, issues are in jeopardy of being sold on the basis of temporary personal exigencies ripping apart a long-term investment position.

Beyond its risk-control feature, a reserve will enable you to aggressively seize advantage from exaggerated market reactions. When events whip market enthusiasm and the bulls romp, one may find the market as a whole and one's own issues becoming overvalued. One may then lighten one's stock holdings and, if there are no attractive alternative issues, add to the reserve. If one reduces one's holdings in an increasingly overvalued market (as described in the chapter on minimizing risk) and adds the proceeds to the reserve, two desirable objectives may be accomplished. First, one may have minimized losses from the subsequent downturn. Second, one now has the cash available to purchase new or previously held issues at reduced prices created by that downturn.

Make the timing of such additions to and subtractions from the reserve according to the standards of value described herein for the purchase and sale of stock. Note that there are unknown risks and gains both ways. In a high market, the risks are the following: (1) loss from a drop on issues still held and (2) gains aborted on issues prematurely sold. In a depressed market, the risks are as follows: (1) loss on issues prematurely bought and (2) lost opportunities for gains from purchases not made.

Recognize and accept that some losses of both kinds will undoubtedly be made. They are worthwhile if by incurring them we first, stave off the more substantial losses possible in a high-risk market and second, simultaneously position ourselves to take advantage of relative bargains available during or after a downturn. In deciding whether to sell in a risky market or buy in an undervalued one, the following principles may help secure favorable long-term results: (1) emphasize acquisition and maintenance of long-term stock ownership; (2) require that an overvaluation of an otherwise good issue be strikingly substantial before selling (the substantiality required should be increased as the reserve increases in proportion to the total portfolio); (3) when considering a purchase and in possession of a large reserve, require no or only a small discount from fair value for purchase; and (4) when considering a purchase, require an increasing discount from fair value as the size of your reserve decreases.

MINIMIZE TRANSACTIONS

It is obvious that the more frequent the transactions, the greater is the siphoning of brokerage commissions. Yet as Maria Scott observes, " . . . brokerage costs are not the only transaction costs involved in a trade. That's because stocks are not bought and sold at the same price: An investor buys stock at the 'ask' price and sells at the 'bid' price . . . The spread between the two is the market-maker's profit, and it is a cost to the investor."[5]

Second, greater frequency of transactions will necessitate earlier and probably greater payment of taxes. Such payments effectively reduce the size of your working assets. Third, the greater the frequency of transactions, the greater the probability of interrupting dividend and interest payments. All of these effects constitute a drain on invested assets and, unless compensated by an equivalent or greater advantage, will erode performance.

<u>Each sale and purchase must improve performance enough to overcome the penalty of transaction costs plus taxes in order to refrain from damaging overall results</u>. Mark Hulbert compared the performance of advisory newsletters' recommended portfolio and subsequent transactions against the hypothetical performance of those newsletters' initial portfolio simply held for the following year. He found that the recommended trades of the advisors impaired results.[6] If newsletter investment advisors do not possess the skill to overcome the costs of trading, should we be more confident of our ability to trade profitably?

PRESERVE PEACE OF MIND

One's investments should have a positive value. Nevertheless, under certain conditions, investing may be so noxious to one's frame of mind as to become a negative experience. Personal distress may overshadow monetary assets. This can happen if you permit yourself to generate emotions about the investments that are destructive to peace of mind, joy, and breadth of perspective.

At the outset, I insinuated that destructive emotional forces may be tempered, modified, avoided, or removed by an individual who is so motivated. I have implied that an investor may be patient, put aside greed, cope with fear, resist ego involvement with his investments, and surmount despair if any of these should happen to prove troublesome. Not only will destructive feelings have a bad effect upon investment results, irrespective of such results, they clash with serenity.

It is easy to suggest that one is able to establish greater peace of mind, but can one? To what extent can we surmount such noxious emotions? To what extent can we conduct ourselves with reasonably objective critical judgment? To what extent can we enhance peace of mind or joy? Immersed in this culture, most of us unthinkingly assume that we are at the mercy of our emotions, not their master.

Fortunately, these objectives appear to be potentially within the investor's grasp. One can exert influence in two distinct directions. First, and least important, one can attempt to reshape the confronting offensive circumstances. Second, one may reshape one's own response to the confronting circumstances. Using the external control, one may hope to achieve major influence. Using the internal control, one may hope to achieve significant mastery.

Changing the Situation

Heed Your Values

Do not invest in enterprises that offend your values, unless you hope thereby to influence that enterprise. As an owner of common stock, you are also an owner of the enterprise and thereby have a vote and policy-influencing position, however minuscule it may be. You can choose to try your influence, but do not be a passive beneficiary to something you find loathsome.

Suit Your Temperament

Find that degree of risk that you prefer. Choose neither investments nor styles of investing that prompt you to generate nagging worry or panic. While on the other hand one does not want to be bored, most people have better places to look for excitement than their savings. Whatever your bent, your tactics can be adjusted to your temperament. You do not have to give up investing, as some people have confided they felt forced to do.

The primary strategy recommended here, taking long-term diversified equity positions buffered by a reserve, stimulates minimal anxiety. One can properly pay little attention to the swings of the market if one wishes. Conversely, using leverage or investing so as to take advantage of short-term market actions presents both greater actual risk and greater preoccupation with the risk.

There are those who crave greater risk-taking than is offered by the strategy presented here. A confident professional, assured of continued income production for all ordinary needs, may be quite happy to throw away a portion of his income if he could thereby gain even a remote chance at striking a fortune. So might a frustrated "big wheel," who, spurning mere sufficiency, is willing to stake all on a chance at a fabulous fortune. Then there are those who depend on role for status and may enjoy the instant transformation they may associate with heady ventures or exotic forms of investment. Others may envision a specific goal that would otherwise be out of reach. Persons with such desires may tailor their tactics toward greater risk. Extreme risk takers might (1) use leverage, (2) participate in venture founding, (3) invest for short-term swings, (4) trade in commodities and options with which they are neither expert nor hedging, or (5) engage in short sales. Following such tactics will in all probability drain all sums ventured, but for some, it may be worth it, especially with a chance for the rainbow.

Mastering Yourself

The idea that we have potential control over our emotions is so contrary to our customary assumptions that it may be supposed that I am talking of something else: emotional suppression. Indeed I am not talking of suppression, but of its opposite, heightened awareness. I hold awareness to be essential. It is important to be aware of our emotions, especially destructive ones. I am talking instead of what we do in producing and shaping our emotions by the assumptions and beliefs that we bring to bear. Our emotions arise from the interplay between our ideas and what we encounter in the real world. With the partial exception of the pain of physical trauma and momentary reactions, what we feel depends upon what we think. If we think according to invalid or arbitrary ideas with which we cause ourselves to be upset, we should examine our ideas. We may want to change those found wanting. We may want to alter those beliefs we find either untrue or simultaneously arbitrary and destructive. Since our beliefs frame our emotions, if we really change the beliefs that we wish to reject, there is evidence to indicate that our emotions will be altered.

Modern American cultural dogmas hold that we are thoroughly molded by one or several of the following: culture, society, class, ethnicity, family, chance, karma, genetic structure, traumatic events, or divine control. We do not think of characteristics like impatience, fearfulness, or circumspection as predispositions or habits that are shaped by partially individually determined beliefs, assumptions, and practice. Of course we have genetic structure, ethnic background, societal membership, and variously good or bad luck in the situations into which we were born. These all exert their distinctive influence on each of us. Nevertheless, these merely subject us to their influence; we are not passive clay.

We respond to these influences according to our beliefs. Since we formed our important governing assumptions and their primary corollary beliefs in infancy, they were preverbal at their inception. From this, three important propositions flow. First, we as distinct individuals are partially independent authors of our own first beliefs. Second, since they are preverbal, we are usually unaware of what our central organizing beliefs are. Third, if we have not specified what they are, we probably never have subjected them to critical inspection, and may therefore be operating by beliefs, some of which we would find untenable or even absurd were we to examine them.

Genetic and environmental influences played a role in shaping us originally and continue to affect us. These may be thought of as setting up limits and inclinations, not as complete determinants. Of course, if one believes they control, then they do. Those who use computers know that we can use the programs' circumstances placed before us or we can write our own programs. Even many proponents of the various viewpoints of external determinism leave escape clauses, which may be expressed variously as free will, anomaly, the Heisenberg uncertainty principle, exception, chance, the apparent versus the real, karma, etc.

The view that emotions and attitudes are shaped by our thoughts and actions and consequently are under our control has endured across thousands of years. Ancient philosophers such as Epictetus[7] and Marcus Aurelius[8] propounded this view and maintained that we have more control over our passions than anything else in life. Cognitive theorists in modern psychology like Kelly[9] and Ellis[10] and those in psychiatry like Beck[11] have argued and provided evidence that we are collaborators in our own continuing emotional misfortunes and thereby we are also empowered to bring about our own relief. The viability of this position is suggested by the successful results with patients, particularly those of Beck and his adherents.[12] Frankl,[13] an Austrian psychiatrist whom the Nazis condemned as a Jewish prisoner in a death camp, provides a striking account of a human being's ultimate control over his own emotional well-being. In spite of the remorseless oppression wielded by the Nazis, he found that the key to his and other prisoners' emotional response lay within themselves. It lay with their interpretation and internal structuring of their lives and position.

This trend in thought from Epictetus to Ellis asserts that the events that happen to us affect us less than our opinions about those events. Ideas that certain events are noxious or hurtful predestine their hurtful impact. When the premises or reasoning supporting the belief is patently fallacious or purely arbitrary, the hurt produced, although needless, is nonetheless painful. The investor can learn, although with effort, to put aside ideas that are either fallacious or destructive and arbitrary. One must first identify the troublesome thoughts. Next one must assess their validity and consider the validity of new alternative ideas. This enables one to try out the new and practice putting aside the destructive. With practice, this becomes progressively easier. I refer those who would like to see this process described in a clear, easy format to Burns's[14] practically-oriented handbook, *Feeling Good*.

Achieving a Blend

The investment strategy outlined here can assist the investor in improving his investment attitudes. The idea that one's stocks must go up and that it is terrible if they go down is simultaneously invalid, arbitrary, and destructive. Yet this attitude plagues many investors. I have suggested an investment strategy that, if followed, would shift the investor's perspective away from short-term price movements toward long-term fundamentals, while strengthening the realization that prices will rise and fall haphazardly along the way. To such an investor, a drop in price is no cause for anxiety, being natural, expected, and nonthreatening. In just such a way someone who is happy with his home may have little concern with the fluctuations of the current real estate market. In addition, as the stock market becomes more extremely valued, whether over or under, strong market movements in either direction provide opportunities, as long as both a reserve and a stock position continue.

The most self-possessed and undisturbed investor realizes that the most he or she can lose is monetary and views this from a realistic and balanced value system. Financial assets are good. In amounts greater than required for food, clothing, shelter, and medical care, they are sources of conveniences, comforts, and extension of activities and presence; but they do not touch the most fundamental aspects of a good life. Without financial riches, pleasures of the senses, affect, and intellect remain. Likewise, opportunity to exercise one's capacities for joyful living, societal contribution, harmonious relatedness, and expansion of awareness remain. Although enhanced by financial assets, beyond the provision of the necessities, such aspects of life are not dependent upon them.

Chapter 11

Criteria for Stock Selection

In describing methods of minimizing particular risks and optimizing benefits, I have mentioned some criteria for stock selection: (1) financial strength, (2) growth, (3) yield, (4) predictability, (5) reasonable cost, (6) and diversity. This was done to portray those topics and also to relate the criteria to specific risks and benefits. With a feel for how each criterion relates to safety, income, and growth, you can fashion a set of criteria to both your own values and the contemporary market situation.

I now wish to present my recommended criteria explicitly as a coherent set by which to select stocks. In accordance with the strategic principle of a multivariate approach, these criteria are all to be used together. Apply them successively in your own order of importance. Admit to a pool of portfolio candidates only those stocks that pass all of the requirements. From this pool, you may select stocks for investment that both conform to portfolio requirements and maximize the features you seek.

As they reflect my own standards, I present these criteria merely as a starting point. Make adjustments so as to accommodate to your particular weighting of values as well as to diverse market situations. When the market is at an ebb and bargains abound, you will find that requirements can be tightened for safety, income, and growth together and still have a sufficient pool of stocks for a portfolio.

These criteria are advanced for investors who want to achieve the following objectives in this order of priorities: (1) preserve capital, (2) promote growth, and (3) provide income. For readers who want greater definition and who recall my description of weighting objectives, these criteria are appropriate to a safety-6 growth-5, and income-4 investor. Investors differing in the priority of their objectives can adjust the criteria accordingly.

The payment of ample dividends restrains real growth because both are largely financed by earnings. As rivals in the division of earnings, the enlargement of one tends to be at the sacrifice of the other, but this inverse relationship between dividend payment and growth is only a tendency. It is not immutably inverse since opportunities for profitable new investment differ widely from company to company. Thus some companies pay generous dividends and grow vigorously, while others fail at both.

The reader should adjust the criteria presented here to suit his or her own balance among the three objectives enumerated above—safety, income, and growth. If you value current income more highly, you would require a higher yield. If this is done with no other adjustments in criteria, the pool of acceptable stocks may be too limited to make up a portfolio. To compensate, other criteria deemed less important can be loosened. If, instead, swift growth is desired, one would raise the desired growth rate and probably choose to lower the required yield.

Whereas with criteria related to safety, almost every stock must meet a uniformly high minimum; with yield and growth, we are more concerned with the portfolio average. For growth rates and yield, therefore, we should have in mind both a minimum criterion and a desired portfolio average. Since selection is by minimum qualifications, the portfolio average will he higher than any of our criteria.

CRITERIA FOR INDIVIDUAL STOCK PURCHASE

Earnings Growth Trend

Since stable growth can protect capital as well as provide the means for increasing both dividend income and stock value, indication of its presence and extent is of prime importance. Remember that the aspect of growth that we are primarily interested in is earnings. Without a stable history of earnings growth, estimating future growth is much more precarious.

Why should we look to history? Do we not want to know what is going to happen rather than what has happened? Nonetheless, long-established patterns tend to recur. Thus history gives the most important first approximation for long-term prediction. I would expect a poker player who has been a consistent winner for several years to prevail again in the future, despite a bust night tonight. Just so, should we heed long-term trends. Although trends may change, just as winning poker players may become senile, it is folly to assume this from a short-term deviation. Lacking a clear reason to set historical norms aside, they deserve scrutiny. Thus the following criteria are advanced:

Magnitude of Earnings Growth

I recommend requiring that a stock have an estimated earnings growth rate in excess of 11% per year. Calculate the estimate growth rate by integrating future and historical rates. A future growth rate predicted by an analyst of a disinterested publication such as Value Line or Standard & Poor's should be averaged with an historical rate. A stabler estimate may be obtained by using more than one of each type of estimate. With an average of 11% or more per year, you may attain a portfolio average of 15% per year.

For the historical rate, look across a number of years both for stability of estimate and to even out possible accounting artifacts. If accounting procedures tend to elevate one year at the expense of others, an average over a span of years will present a better picture of operational growth. If more than one historical rate is used, calculate them by different indices or across different time spans. Using a span shorter than the most recent five years risks impairing representativeness, while going beyond sixteen years to calculate the average rate risks diminished relevancy. Of course, if one can show an average rate in excess of 11% across the past five years, ten years, and also across the past sixteen, that may simply reinforce the picture of stability.

Note that earnings growth rates broadly fluctuate according to a number of factors such as inflation during the recent past, the climate of business optimism or pessimism, the tightness or expansion of the money supply, etc. Therefore, acceptable growth rates will vary across time. If we retained the 11% standard when growth rates generally are dampened, we would be in danger of so reducing our pool of acceptable stocks that we might not have enough to pass all of our criteria. So view this figure as a tentative one to be varied as circumstances dictate. At present, given the dismal financial outlook, I would suggest that an estimated growth rate of 9% per year for the ensuing five years would be more appropriate than 11%. Looking back over the past five years, a growth rate of 11% is a good standard; if it continues back to ten or fifteen years, so much the better.

In estimating earnings growth rates, a key desideratum is the ability to stay ahead of inflation by about 4% to 9%. This may be used to adjust the required earnings rate. Of course if growth rates are generally much higher when we are looking to invest, we can take advantage of that by raising our minimum required.

You can use the historical growth figure published by an advisory service or calculate it yourself from earnings data. The assistance of a calculator or computer makes this quite easy. Divide the last year's earnings by the first year's. Next, extract the root of this number that is one less than the number of years under review. Finally, subtract one to find the average annual growth. For example, Growth Inc. earned $5.00 per share last year and $1.00 per share ten years ago. $5.00 divided by $1.00 equals 5. The ninth root of 5 is 1.1958132. Subtract 1 and round to 1958, which is 19.58%. If either the first or last years are unusually low or high, one may instead use an average of the first three and last three, remembering to appropriately decrease the root to be extracted. A third method of calculation is to take an average of the yearly percentage increase figures. Agreement between the methods indicates stability in the growth rate.

In addition to calculating growth directly from earnings per share, it is instructive to look at the yearly percentage increase in the common equity. Over a span of time, the average of the two should converge. The latter figures are perhaps more indicative of the directors' policy to sustain growth.

Stability of Earnings Growth

An advisory service rating for earnings predictability should place the company no lower than the top fourth of companies that it reviews. Increases in yearly earnings should have occurred in at least twelve of the past sixteen years. During years of nongrowth, the average yearly loss should be no more than 15%. Accept no more than three consecutive nongrowth years. Should any stagnant years have occurred in the past five, consider the reasons for the impairment of growth in order to rule out the likelihood of a negative shift to the long-term trend.

Nonetheless, when evaluating a potential bargain because of a turnaround situation, you may allow greater latitude. The reason for the instability and its turnaround should be sufficiently clear to instill comfort in projecting a future uptrend. The situation of oil companies in 1986 is a case in point.

Future Prospects

You will want some assurance to sustain confidence that the growth trend may continue in the future. Here you may have to rely primarily upon analysts' ratings and reports. Although, you may also wish to exercise your own judgment about the economic factors facing the company and the direction and magnitude of change that these may occasion. Specifically you may wish to require the following:

a. Analysts' estimate of future growth should be no less than 11% per year for the next three-to-five-year period. While a minimum of 11% per year is the relevant criterion for stock selection, 15% is the target for the portfolio average. The figure may go down in a depressed general market.

b. You should have some confidence that the company's prosperity will continue. Should any cloud suggestive of danger to the company's future appear, it should either be temporary, insignificant, or be judged to be fully compensated for by a depressed market price. *Insignificant* here means that even if the danger came to pass, one's minimal criteria would still be met.

Safety

Financial Strength

Analysts' Ratings

The financial strength of the company should be rated within the top fourth of companies reviewed. A Value Line or Standard & Poor's rating of A—or better satisfies this requirement.

Adequacy of Cash Flow

Cash flow (income plus accounting charges against income that do not require the expenditure of cash, as depreciation, amortization, and depletion) should be large enough to pay dividends, finance capital replacement needs, and provide an excess for new investment. While other financial aspects such as ease of debt coverage and adequacy of working capital (the excess of current assets over current liabilities) will be encompassed within analysts' ratings of financial strength, adequacy of cash flow to finance new investment may not be.

Volatility

Volatility of a stock's market price presents a risk to the investor. For a long-term perspective, this risk may not be all that great, but if your need for cash coincides with an extremely bad market reaction, volatile stocks may be regretted. I would seek a portfolio average beta of .90 to 1. As a criterion for individual stock selection, I would accept a stock with a beta of less than 1.5.

Price

Buy no overpriced stock. For the quality of stock indicated above, the C ratio should be 1.3 or lower. That is, the stock's P/E should be no more than 1.3 times the sum of its expected growth plus its yield. A stock of superlative characteristics, easily surpassing all the minimal requirements above, may be bought with a C ratio of 1.4. Of course, it would be better with a C of 0.5. Before the 1982 bull market began, there was a plethora of superior-quality stocks with C ratios around or below 0.75.

Use the other valuation models as well. Do not exceed the value of the Graham model given earlier. I rely heavily on a model that discounts future receipts by projecting earnings according to a calculated growth rate. My rate combines future growth rate estimates by analysts together with historical growth rates. Then I adjust the rate according to (1) the trend of the change in the earnings growth rate and (2) an estimate for future degradation of the growth rate. This may sound like great deal of work, but with a computer, one just does this once on a spreadsheet. Then you only have to fill in the appropriate data for earnings, dividends, predictability, financial strength, and desired discount rate. Do not exceed the value yielded by this projection.

A lucky investor may find him—or herself awash in capital ready for investment. If reserves are substantial and attractive investment alternatives in other markets absent, the price limits derived from the various value models may be nudged slightly upward. If, in addition, neither the economy nor the stock market is showing signs of excess, one may raise them somewhat more. There may be more to be lost here from opportunities not taken than from excessive price, especially if these higher prices are at long-term market average. One of the points of usefulness of the C ratio and the other value models is the protection from buying into an inflated market. Therefore, one should not allow the inflation of the market to influence the tolerable level of C much above these market average points. A C of 1.5 is overpriced. If the market contains no stock meeting the other criteria that is not above 1.5, then the market is too inflated for further purchase.

Dividends

Magnitude

Paying dividends sacrifices some growth potential. Growth-minded investors, therefore, may be content with a modest yield. Nonetheless, there are three reasons I would not want to settle for a low yield. First, as growth rates soar up past 20% per year, the prices asked for that extra growth rate are exorbitant. In contrast, an approximately equal performance of 16% growth and 4% yield is not likely to have attracted much attention on either account. Consequently it may be comparatively cheap. Second, you receive dividend payments each quarter, whereas the fruits of growth may not be received. The saying, "A bird in the hand is worth two in the bush," would not have become trite without more than a little truth. Third, the fruits of growth are received as capital gain. The tax is applied not just to real gains but to historical inflation as well. Thus, it's possible that you might be paying tax on a loss of value. Growing dividends sidestep this burden.

I set my criterion for a stock's yield at 1.2%. That is less than half of the desired portfolio yield on stocks at about 3%. To illustrate the change wrought by altered market conditions, in 1982 these figures were 1.75% and 4.25%. As there are some superlative stocks with low yields, I am willing to entertain some fairly low yields, but I would not want to go too low for the reasons given.

Continuity of Growth

If you want growing income, as I recommend, assure yourself that dividends are growing along with earnings. Where dividends have been growing in pace with or slightly behind earnings, there is indication of a policy to provide continual growth in dividends. Such a policy when connected with an estimate of earnings growth gives you a basis for predicting dividend growth.

Be leery of a pronounced deviation in the rate of dividend growth from the rate of earnings growth, regardless of the direction of the deviation. Where dividends diverge toward a substantially slower growth than earnings without an explanation such as holding funds for an unforeseen new investment, either (1) earnings growth is accelerating while dividend growth is maintained at a previous level or (2) profitability is declining and management is compensating by cutting dividend growth. Management might try to maintain earnings growth by allowing a smaller division of income to dividends. If this is happening, look to see if it's arising from a deteriorating position or from a long lag time connected with the profitability of a new venture. Where dividends are growing much faster than earnings, you might question the company's eventual ability to sustain growth through new investment. If significant, such concerns are likely to be addressed by an analyst's report on the stock.

CRITERIA FOR PORTFOLIO CONSTRUCTION AND MAINTENANCE

After having applied the above criteria for individual stock selection, one has a pool of stocks that, having passed all minimum requirements, are candidates for inclusion in the portfolio. Between twenty and twenty-eight candidates is ideal. If one has much below or above that number, one could try a slight alteration of the criteria. Should more candidates be desired, one could try easing the criterion deemed least important. One could, for example, shift the beta requirement from 1.5 to 1.75 or even drop it altogether. One could loosen two or three criteria together. On the other hand, if we want fewer stocks, one would tighten the criterion we deem most important or tighten to a lesser extent the two or three most important.

From this pool, our task is now to select the specific stocks we want in the amounts that we want. We should make this final selection and determination in light of the following considerations:

Diversify the Risks

Across Companies

Tailor the portfolio so that sources of risk are optimally dispersed. Since one source of risk is company specific, invest in a number of companies. There are two reasons for this. The first reason is conveyed by the saying, "Don't put all your eggs in one basket!" Inadequate diversification across companies increases the percentage of value in jeopardy by one adverse occurrence. Clearly, investing in just one company magnifies the total risk, since a single negative occurrence would strike the entire portfolio. The second reason is that the opportunity for countervailing influence is reduced.

I submit that the optimal number of stocks for a portfolio is between sixteen and twenty-five.

You must balance two opposing values. On the one hand, the more stocks held, the more blunt the advantage of selectivity. On the other hand, small numbers increase portfolio risk. When very few stocks are held, the addition of one more appreciably lowers the portfolio risk. As you keep on adding stocks, the additional advantage from decreasing risk gets smaller and smaller. Fewer than twenty tends to tangibly increase the company-specific risk. While above twenty-eight, increases do very little to minimize risk.

So somewhere in this range seems appropriate. My tendency would be to take twenty-three as a starting target figure. I would be able to move upward or downward within this range, by the appeal, or lack thereof, of the prospective candidates. I would also allow this figure to be modified downward by the exigencies of a small portfolio. A $10,000 portfolio composed of twenty issues is an average of $500, which necessitates a substantially larger percent of one's capital paid out for commissions. This is particularly true when dealing with a full-service broker who, in addition to generally higher charges, adds a special odd lot charge. In such a case, in order to avoid the cramping of growth, which the larger commissions will cause, I would prefer to cut the number of stocks down to perhaps as low as six. The use of a discount broker who does not charge for odd lots is a major advantage to an investor in this category. Alternatively, where the amount to be invested will not support fifteen or sixteen round lots (below around $40,000), one may consider using a mutual fund to achieve proper diversification. Unfortunately, doing this, you will be increasing costs and removing your ability to guide the investment.

Across Other Nonsystematic Sources of Risk

Although company-specific risks are contained by controlling the number of stocks, other sources of nonsystematic risk remain, which also need to be contained by diversification. These include the industrial and regional sources of risk. While a selection of twenty bank stocks would take care of company systematic risk, it would leave one extremely vulnerable to events affecting the industry as a whole. Therefore, the stocks should also represent a diversity of industries.

A portfolio of stocks embracing companies such as a sugar plantation, bank, newspaper, electric utility, construction company, grocery chain, hotel, and department store may sound well diversified, but if they all happen to be Hawaiian, they are all vulnerable to some common risks. A strike of stevedores could simultaneously imperil all of them. The same could happen by a drop in tourism, a drought, a devastating hurricane, a realignment of military forces, or any other single blow to the local economic base. Clearly, diversification should also reach across industrial, regional, and other sources of nonsystematic risk.

Weighting of Stocks

The exposition above assumes an approximately equal amount invested in each issue. Clearly, if one has 90% of the portfolio invested in one stock and the other 10% invested in nineteen stocks, one has no more than a token scattering of risk. One should generally aim at an approximately equal weighting.

Nevertheless, if you wish some representation in a more risky area, you may choose deliberately to decrease the exposure by investing a smaller amount. If you are interested in an industry with overall good prospects, but high company-specific risk, you may choose to give that industry the normal weighting but spread that industry holding across small amounts of a few stocks.

Shape Portfolio Attributes

Another exception to equal weighting comes from the attempt to shape particular portfolio characteristics from a selected pool of stocks. For example, to achieve a desired portfolio yield, one might slightly lower the representation in lower-yielding stocks to heighten the effect of the higher yields. One could follow this procedure for other single attributes that one wanted to emphasize—for example, growth. Then again, one could do this for combinations of attributes such as predictable growth (an index derived from multiplying an index of predictability of growth by the growth rate) or any other blending of characteristics one might want to maximize. If one wished, one could then attempt to do this with a second characteristic or blend of characteristics. In this way, one could transform the pool of potential stocks into a portfolio design that both adequately limits nonsystematic risk and optimizes the investor's desired attributes.

In emphasizing some stocks and slighting others, do not stray from adequate diversification. Adding more than twenty stocks will enable you to slight some without increasing the representation in others too much. Do not purchase a holding in one company greater than 8% of the portfolio without a special reason, such as your funds are too limited.

Respond to Altered Circumstances

As time passes, circumstances will change. Market values will inflate or deflate. You may be pleased with some of your issues and disappointed in others. You may learn of issues not previously noticed. Previously dismissed issues may have fundamentally changed. Periodic review is important to both minimize risks and maximize benefits. Situations will appear prompting consideration of purchase or sale.

Within Your Portfolio

With time, some stocks will grow in value more than others, and consequently unequal weighting will result. This is of no real consequence if kept within bounds. When representation in individual stocks exceeds around 10%, the risk containment benefits of the portfolio are beginning to erode. If one has twenty stocks, but one issue is worth 20% of the portfolio, that is excessive. The issue's prospects and risks should be reviewed and a partial sale considered. However, do not automatically discard a stable and rising issue just because it is outperforming your others.

Outside Your Portfolio

Fluctuations in price relative to value incessantly occur, and at times, extremes will be reached. Dangers and opportunities constantly change as prices change. Ignore small fluctuations, but if extreme, evaluate a shift across markets.

CRITERION FOR STOCK SALES

Personal desires or exigencies may lead to withdrawing funds from one's savings. Of such sales, I will say two things. First, have a cash reserve to provide such funds so as not to force an inopportune sale. Second, if you must sell, do it so as to minimize damage to the quality and prospects of the portfolio after taxes.

The rest of this section is concerned with those sales made for investment purposes. For a variety of reasons, you may feel that you can better advance your fortunes by switching the stocks or markets in which you invest. A few things should be considered before leaping.

<u>Dominant Criterion for Sales</u>

If you want to sell to buy another stock, determine if by making the transfer, your long-term portfolio value will increase beyond the sum of transaction costs.

Transaction Costs

Sales have cash consequences that cannot be ignored. These costs may include, among other things, federal taxes, state taxes, brokerage commissions, SEC fees, load charges, interruption of dividend flow, and the discrepancy between bid and ask prices. Income tax consequences are the most important. Make an estimate of your gain and its tax consequence. Do not be lulled into thinking the cost is whatever the federal rate for gains is at the moment. There may also be state taxes. Depending on your resulting income level, there may be additional increases in taxes as (1) deductions and exemptions are lost, (2) the alternative minimum tax is called into play, and (3) penalties are imposed because your earlier estimated tax payments were made without knowledge of this addition.

On top of the above transaction's costs, when you reinvest your funds, you will pay another brokerage fee. This transfer makes no sense unless you believe that the smaller amount in stock B is worth more than the larger amount in stock A across your time horizon.

Since a large part of long-term gains represents an adjustment to inflation, the tax may weigh more heavily upon the illusion of profits than upon their reality. It is now quite possible that what at first appeared to be a substantial profit may actually be a real loss. Without a system to adjust gains for inflation, many people will pay income taxes for transactions on which they have actually suffered a loss of value. This applies potentially to all investments, including your home.

<u>Possible Reasons Prompting Sales</u>

Excessive Price Increase

Do not take profits merely because your holding has risen in price. When the price increase can no longer be justified by the underlying value, then reexamine to evaluate the appropriateness of selling.

Stock Market Overpricing

In chapter 9, "Tactics of Minimizing Risks," I treated overpricing at some length regarding minimizing systematic market risk. The standards presented there apply to marketwide overvaluation where the whole market's rising tide lifts your issues along with the rest. If your stocks and tax situation warrant selling, you may consider some pruning in overvalued markets. Market average benchmark figures to use as rough guidelines in cutting stock representation to a level of 80% of portfolio are the following: C moves above 1.64, P/E rises above 18, and yield sinks below 2.74. Deeper retrenchment was suggested for consideration as benchmarks become more aberrant.

In considering the above, please note three things. First, I have presented merely some objective signs of market overpricing to use as guidelines. Quantitative indices like C, P/E, measures of absolute value, and percentage yield are extremely important in tracking how bloated or attractive prices have become and for use as prompts for purchase or sale. However, never use them without a qualitative look. Review the prevailing situation. Is there an explanation for what is happening that should prompt you to reconsider? Have the underlying values changed? Compare the attractiveness of alternative markets and of different stock issues with your particular issues. Nevertheless, do not ignore what the indices of value are telling you.

Second, although I speak of three benchmarks, I use these only as points on a continuum of increasing market overpricing. The investor's response should be slow starting, but gradually accelerating. Ignore minimal overpricing. Respond to moderate overpricing minimally. Respond to moderately high overpricing moderately, but respond extremely to extreme overvaluation.

Third, the figures above refer to market averages, not the investor's own stocks. You presumably will have equivalently inflated prices, possibly even higher because of higher-than-average quality. In selecting which of your own stocks to sell in response to systematic market extremity, employ the following guides: (1) prune out your weakest and most vulnerable issues, (2) minimize the tax consequences, and (3) restore adequate distribution. Your own portfolio will tell you which of these to emphasize.

Selective Overpricing

Some of your holdings may become selectively overpriced within a fairly priced market. Your first indices of this are market prices that exceed 1.3 times the indices of absolute value, 1.3 times the Graham Value, 1.5 times the Sharp Value, or a C elevated above 1.5. As the indices get larger, the urgency of reassessment becomes clearer. Should they reach 2 or above, take action. Look at the indices individually and averaged together. Look to see if one index is responding to a potential unrecognized by the others. Before selling, look for what might have prompted the selective market response. An advisory service is often quite helpful here. The market's reaction could be an adjustment to a change in underlying value. Revised estimates of growth or quality may be in order. If so, amend your calculations of objective indices.

Next, look to see if you want to take your profits. Is there an attractive alternative investment? Will the tax consequence of the prospective sale help or hinder you, and how importantly? After considering this, make your judgment. You may sell everything, sell a portion, or decide to hold unless a given point is reached.

Deterioration of Value

Deterioration will probably first be evident upon a portfolio review, a falling price, or possibly from information disseminated as news or advice. First, evaluate the situation. What is the probable cause? How great does the damage to the company seem to be? Is this a single blow with a temporary effect, or does it presage a declining path? Compare your assessment, error-prone though it may be, with the effect upon the market price.

The market may have overreacted to a single occurrence, and the issue may then be attractively underpriced. Johnson & Johnson was hit by lethal tampering of a major product, not only once but twice. The company responded strongly, chose safety above immediate cost, restructured the packaging and recovered. By throwing its unstinting support to prevent a recurrence, the company not only managed to make the packaging safer, but to reestablish itself. In the depth of its trouble, the investor would have done better to stand by the company.

Likewise, Freeport Sulphur stock was hit hard after the communist government took power in Cuba. Rumors were rife of a nationalization of its Cuban facility, and the stock's price was battered. However, even the outright loss of the asset and the income generated by it were not sufficiently large to justify the market's reaction. Again, the undaunted investor came off well.

However, perhaps more frequently, the problem is deeply entrenched and likely not only to continue, but to worsen. More often the problem is not a single incident, but an emerging flaw in the company's operations, costs, or markets. Do not hesitate to cut your losses if this is your estimate.

Chapter 12

Getting Started

PRELIMINARY DECISIONS

Whether you are just now preparing to invest or have long since begun, some basic decisions should be crystallized. These decisions will probably suit you best if you make them yourself. There are a few hustling brokers, editors, and advisors who may thrust themselves upon you and try to put you into a preconceived mold. If you want to feel comfortable, make your own basic decisions about how you wish to proceed. Some investors will be tempted to let someone else take responsibility, but responsibility unavoidably stays with the investor, as one thereby will have given preliminary endorsement to whatever is decided that is not legally actionable.

Set Your Objectives

By now you may have clarified your investment objectives. If not, take the time to state them to your satisfaction. Without a consistent sense of your goals, you will have no reference by which to set your selection criteria. Between preservation, income, and growth, which is your first priority, which is your second? How strongly does your first priority overshadow your second and third, and your second overshadow your third?

If income is important, would you like it designed to be plentiful, reliable, or growing? How would you weigh these subsidiary objectives for income? If growth is important, do you want it to be maximal or reliable? How much risk is acceptable? If safety is important, do you want to preserve nominal or real value?

Decide on Your Participation

Do you want to make investment decisions by yourself, or would you feel more comfortable having someone else make them for you? If you want to make decisions yourself, do you want to advise yourself, receive advice from others, or both?

Several alternatives confront you. You may hire an investment manager, which may be an individual or a trust company. You may hire an investment consultant who advises, but leaves decisions up to you. You may utilize a broker as a manager or advisor if you wish. You may invest in one or more mutual funds, where you choose the nature of the funds, but everything else is necessarily delegated to fund managers. You may make your own decisions on information you obtain and which you may or may not recast to suit your strategy. Knowing the degree you wish to participate will enable you to achieve the most comfortable arrangement. Your decision will hinge on your time available, desires, confidence, and wealth.

To invest successfully does not mean mastery of all of the arcane instruments and methods available. It is much more important to have a clear, though elementary, grasp of the subject; this means an appreciation of risks and benefits, a coherent strategy based upon fundamentals, an understanding of your objectives, and a bit of self knowledge and control. This does not remove all risk. Things may go wrong, even for the expert, for the venture is into future possibility, not certainty.

Decide on Your Sources of Information

No matter how you proceed, you need information. If you have decided to turn your investment decisions over to someone else, then you will assume that you need not worry about information. If you use an advisor, you may or may not want supplementary information. If you act on your own, a source of reliable and timely information is indispensable. In this case, I recommend a full-service publication like the *Value Line Investment Survey*. Standard & Poor's the *Outlook*, which provides less information but good conservative advice supplemented by some of its other services, is an alternative. If you use a newsletter, I recommend that it be only as a supplement, unless you wish to slavishly follow its advice. I have not yet seen a newsletter that gave enough information to allow the reader to establish an independent opinion.

State Your Strategy

If you do not attempt to formulate your strategy in at least rough terms, peculiar changes could occur without your awareness. You could wind up like the broker who having said that he believes in long-term investing on fundamentals went on to say, "This stock is losing favor, so it looks like it's going to drop in the next few weeks. Sell now! You'll have extra profits to invest." Not only premises may be contradictory, but important ramifications may be ignored.

I am not saying that strategy should not be changed. Rather, let us keep a healthy skepticism toward our own ideas and hold them open to change should the evidence warrant. Don't let yourself slip into considering that they are absolute certainties, which they can never be. Treating them as tentative hypotheses rather than absolute certainties will serve us better, produce less mischief, and provide the only graceful avenue to growth of understanding. Nevertheless, a change in strategy should come from a decision that it is appropriate to shift, not from inattention, conformity, or fuzziness.

SUGGESTED PRIORITIES FOR THE STAGES OF LIFE

Your situation in life may influence your investment priorities. Across one's life span, priorities tend to shift from growth in youth to preservation in middle age and finally to income in old age. If you are accumulating something for your preschool children or grandchildren, growth will probably be uppermost, while funds for yourself or your parents may be invested quite differently.

For young adults, it is most helpful to start first with building up a cash equivalent reserve. However, if there are people dependent on one person who is earning, then that person should protect his dependents with term life insurance. What is important here is the protection afforded by insuring your earning capacity for your dependents. With a whole life policy, there is an extra benefit, clearly visible as you near retirement, which represents something besides insuring your earning capacity. That part of such a policy represents an investment and, as such, should be considered from the alternative risk benefit standpoint presented here. In the face of incessant inflation, the excess in a whole life policy that represents an investment is likely to be a poor one.

Next, young adults would probably be best advised to buy a home as early as can be advantageously done, providing they plan to live there for a few years. Above the provision for a necessity, there is a layer of inflation protection topped with the frosting of multiple entrenched tax advantages. It is one of the few cakes that you can simultaneously eat and yet keep.

Taking Charge

The option is yours; you can take charge of your savings or not. Taking charge does not mean doing everything yourself; you can delegate and still be in charge. Instead, taking charge is adopting an attitude of responsibility. This refers to acceptance of accountability; this is the source of your power to influence events. Without taking charge, even with earnings large enough to produce luxury, you may be unable to put aside the first dollar with which to start your savings.

The source of your investments is savings. The source of your savings is your decision to put aside some of your earnings for use in future contingencies. The source of that decision is the attitude of responsibility toward self and others whom you support. This attitude is manifest by taking charge.

If you would like to take charge and make your own decisions, but hesitate to do so because you lack confidence, take heart from studies that suggest that people who express greater confidence in their abilities do not have greater ability than those who express less confidence.[1] The expression of confidence appears to be a personality trait much more importantly than an indication of ability or correctness.[2] Indeed, there is evidence to suggest that those who express extreme confidence have inefficient patterns of thinking in that they tend toward rigidity and dogmatism.[3] So whether or not you feel up to it, and whether or not you would delegate investment decisions, I invite you to take charge. If you hand your money over to someone else to manage, prudence dictates some oversight.

You need not be an investment expert unless you try to squeeze out extra money by unusual or risky manipulations. Basic elementary knowledge, sufficient emotional control to enable your judgment to prevail, and willingness to take charge should serve you well. As Benjamin Graham, the investment analyst and author, said, "Have the courage of your knowledge and experience . . . To achieve satisfactory investment results is easier than most portfolio realize; to achieve superior results is harder than it looks."[4]

PART V

OVERVIEW AND OUTLOOK

Chapter 13

Market Depressions, Recessions, and Booms

The various markets (stocks, bonds, real estate, gold, etc.) continually fluctuate. At times, the alterations are severe; and we have a depression, a recession, or a surging boom.

In common stocks, there are several possible causes of the fluctuations. For example: oversupply of production, crop failures, increased cost of basic resources, money supply, strikes, etc. Normally, market forces make a correction, and there is no cause for much consternation. But occasionally non-market forces intrude and hamper the market forces. This is usually in the form of government intervention, which instigates the deepening of a minor recession into a prolonged recession or into a depression, destroying jobs and companies.

1. The Depression of 1907

Following major liquidity problems that had caused an economic slowdown, a panic spread on Wall Street when two men tried to corner the copper market. There were several runs on large banks causing bank doors to close and unemployment to rise. The markets and economy were severely down. The government did not interfere, and the economy and stock prices recovered rather quickly.

2. The Depression of 1921

This depression was due to the inflation produced by funding the First World War. It too was deep, experiencing a decline of 47% from onset to nadir. However, with President Harding's laissez-faire policy, no government intervention occurred; and it recovered within eighteen months.

3. The Great Depression of the 1930s

As the 1921 depression was having a good recovery, the Federal Reserve expanded the money supply. A positive outlook bloomed across the population of the United States and other countries. Consumption and production soared as most looked forward to a future with low unemployment, new opportunities, and wealth. New products like automobiles and aircraft were burgeoning. But the expanded money supply led to an unsustainable credit-driven boom of asset prices in stocks, bonds, and capital goods that tipped the economy downward.

On October 4, 1929, the stock market crashed with prices falling up to 20% in one day. In June 1930, the Smoot-Hawley Tariff was enacted, raising tariffs on imports with duties that reached 50%. In natural response, other countries raised their tariffs, sharpening the drop of American production. Unemployment reached 25%. At its depth, stock prices dropped by 90% from the 1929 highs.

The Federal Reserve reversed itself and held to a tight money policy strangling available credit for the business expansion necessary for job growth. This was the second major cause of the lingering depression.

In 1935, Social Security was enacted. Although the tax rate was small to begin with, it was a new tax spread across most wage earners and was not deductible from their income taxes. In addition, the act imposed a similar tax on all employees to be paid by the employer. Furthermore, it imposed a burden on all employers to handle the accounts of their employees, creating additional costs to eat up the funds available for job creation.

It must be recognized that the government's money comes by extracting it from the people. It has been argued that the costs imposed by Social Security and the several job-creation programs outweighed the economic benefit to the economy from the wages of the workers. Thus, although programs like Social Security and job creation gave help to people in need, they led to the perpetuation with its deprivation of jobs.

In summary, it is fair to say that the Federal Government not only caused the depression but also fueled its persistence. The depression ended with the demands of World War II.

4. Stagflation of the 1970's

In 1971, President Nixon initiated wage and price controls creating an upset to the economy that pushed commodity prices higher and restricted economic freedom and growth. Then in 1973 OPEC raised oil prices that shocked the economy with rising prices on everything that had to be transported. This led to a period of a stagnant economy and inflation. During this period stock prices naturally joined in the sluggishness. Unemployment increased. Labor contracts established cost-of-living clauses, which forced prices to rise. The government followed suit, and prices corkscrewed upward. As jobs were lost while inflation kept prices from crashing, one might call it an invisible recession.

In the late 1970's, President Carter sought to solve the unemployment by increasing government spending. This increased inflation. In 1979 the Federal Reserve Board tightened the money supply to stop inflation. This caused interest rates to soar and slowed business borrowing. The economy dropped into a deeper recession with increased unemployment.

In 1982 and 1983 President Reagan began to cut taxes and deregulate many industries that had been under tight government control. In 1982 the recession remained deep throughout the year, but by 1983 inflation ceased, the economy recovered, unemployment dropped, and the stock market zoomed upward.

5. The Market Crash of 1987

On Monday October 19, 1987, the stock markets of the United States and many other countries plunged sharply, spreading pandemonium in their wake. Following a gradually accelerating decline of stock prices over the previous weeks and concerns over (1) rising interest rates, (2) resurgence of inflation, and (3) the trade deficit, the Dow Jones Industrial Average fell over 22% on "Black Monday." Other indices here and abroad fell in tandem.

Since people above the age of fifty-five had lived with the Great Depression, suicide erupted together with shock, panic, and anger. Many who had gambled heavily on the continuation of the market's upward course were confronted by demands for payment that they could not meet. Many brokerage firms were alarmed about possible insolvency from uncovered margins, and some did fold. With a real estate slump, many savings-and-loans failed. An impending recession was rumored.

Contrary to the general raucous alarm, the sharp drop in market prices was not especially surprising. Rather, it was generally predictable. Those who hold views similar to those espoused in this book would likely have expected such a possibility. In the last two months of 1929, the market fell 47%. The date of a fall was not predictable; nevertheless, the odds of such a drop happening sometime in 1987 or 1988 were daily visibly mounting. By August, the average P/E ratio of the Value Line Industrial Composite reached 17.9. [1] Its average yield reached 2.3%,[1] and the average C was 1.5. While these figures were not extraordinarily high historically, they were high enough to put one on alert and to warrant risk-reduction evaluations.

Investors who used the strategy recommended here suffered no harm. To the contrary, they may have benefited. There are seven reasons why such investors would have come through unscathed. First, they had a significant cash reserve, possibly augmented somewhat as the market rose. Thus, (a) they would not have been forced to sell unwisely and (b) their holdings would have fallen less heavily than they had risen. Second, they were poised to take advantage of a fallen market. Third, since all purchases were made at a reasonable cost, they had few or no purchases in the preceding year and a half, except perhaps for some bargain situations or more defensive positions. Thus, even after the crash, their values would have exceeded their costs by a healthy margin. Fourth, having invested with an eye to financial strength had the crash led into a depression, they would have selected companies unlikely to collapse. Fifth, having invested for the long term, they not only expected market drops and positioned themselves financially and psychologically to live with market lows. Sixth, their attitudes would have been oriented toward a calm acceptance of market gyrations. Seventh, by avoiding time-bound investing, such as buying on margin, they were spared the necessity of taking unnecessary losses.

7. The Current Recession

To pull the economy out of the 2002 recession brought on by the aftereffects of the 9/11 terrorist attacks, the Federal Reserve lowered interest rates. However, the Federal Reserve allowed them to remain low and generated easy credit-based money that as time went on created an unsustainable boom. Thus a stage was set for a bust should a difficulty arise to prick the ballooning bubble.

The immediate trigger for this recession was the rise in oil prices that began a rapid acceleration in 2007. In September 2007, the stock market entered a decline from which it has still not recovered. Unlike the sharp drop of 1987, the drop in prices proceeded gradually for eleven months as the increases in the price of oil slowed the American economy. Then in August 2008, the plight of the housing market became visible and the market took a sharper drop.

The cause of the housing problem was the desire of several politicians, led by President Clinton, to secure affordable housing for low-income persons. Sallie Mae and Freddie Mac, being partly government controlled, were told to accept new loans from banks at substandard rates so that houses could be made available for those who had not the resources to meet bank standards. Banks were urged by them to make those loans as Sallie Mae and Freddie Mac would take them over. This urging encouraged banks to pay little attention to the level of risk as they were not the ones to be held responsible. An act by the 106th Congress led to over-leveraging as banks and other financial companies were eager to achieve high rates of return on these packaged substandard loans.

Although the Bush administration saw the substandard loans as a danger to the economy and tried to halt them, the Democrat congress led by Barney Frank, in an apparent desire to help low income housing, refused any change. Thus with the trigger of high oil prices, those having taken substandard loans were unable to meet their payments.

As prices of homes fell, the value of the substandard loan homes were less than the required mortgage payments, and the poor for whom the loans were intended to help were evicted and saddled with debt. Banks, insurance and investment companies that had bought into the packaged mortgage-backed derivatives were on the verge of collapse. In a few months, the market dropped by over 30%.

6. The Outlook

The Obama administration and Congress have been zealously interfering with the free market. Wealth has been transferred out of the private sector and infused into government programs. A job created in the private sector may well spur the development of more jobs. A job created by government drains from the private sector and may destroy other jobs. Programs like the stimulus, cap and trade, and placing the medical system under the control of the government are likely to not only extend the recession but also deepen it into a depression. Although the stimulus bill was enormous, only a very small portion of it was directed toward stimulation of the economy.

Note that in the previous economic downfalls and market drops, recovery came swiftest to those that left the market alone except for reducing taxes, which encourages job growth. Those drops in which government interfered became deeper and prolonged. Throughout recent history, government attempts to produce social and economic change have produced unintended consequences that have been harmful. Such outcomes have been called black swans. Situations like the War on Poverty producing greater poverty, prohibition producing organized crime, minimum wages throwing people out of work, vast sums spent on education producing a less-educated populace, and mandatory seat belt laws leading to increased fatalities of pedestrians, bicyclists, and motorcyclists are too numerous to list.

It appears that the complexities of social and economic affairs are too great to be understood even by experts. Thus the occurrence of Black Swans, and the collapse of economic systems. Witness the demise of the Soviet Union occasioned by economic insufficiency and the junking of Chairman Mao's economic system by his successor, Chairman Deng.

In a free market, decisions are made by millions of individuals and companies who are experts in their own little part of the vast economy. The work of these individual decision makers is weaved together for the good of the whole as each follows his goal of profit making.

Unless a change takes place in government to change the current schemes, few jobs will be created and the economy will sink deeper, bringing poverty to many. With the creation of so much money for the various programs, inflation will arise not long after economic leveling has occurred. That inflation can only be halted by a sharp rise in interest rates that would thrust the economy into a deeper downward spiral.

But at some time, things will change. Current government activities may be altered or things may settle into an impoverished stability. Those who rely on cash or cash denominated assets will be in trouble. Those whose assets are in good-quality stocks, in real estate, or in basic resources will have a hard time for awhile but will likely persevere.

References

Chapter 1

1. Janis, I.L., *Decision Making*, New York: The Free Press, 1977, pg 45

2. Shakespeare, W., *A Midsummer Night's Dream*, v, i, In Durham, W. H., (Ed), The Yale Shakespeare, New Haven, Connecticut: Yale University Press, 1918, pg 64

3. Bruner, J. and Goodman, C., "Value and need as organizing factors in perception". *Journal of abnormal & social psychology*, 1947, 42, pgs 33-44

4. Chronbach, L.J., *Essentials of Psychological Testing*. New York: Harper & Brothers, 1960

5. Kelly, G.A., *The Psychology of Personal Construct*. New York: W.W. Norton, 1955

6. Ibid. Volume 1, pg 516

7. Sheriff, M., "Group influences upon the formation of norms and attitudes". In Newcomb, T.M. and Hartley, E.L. (Eds.), *Readings in social psychology*. New York: Holt, 1947

8. Brown, R., *Social Psychology*. New York: The Free Press, 1965, pg 669

9. Asch, S.E., "Studies of independence and conformity. A minority of one against a unanimous majority". *Psychological Monographs*; 1956, 70, no. 9

10. Kelly, G.A., *The Psychology of Personal Constructs.* New York: W.W. Norton, 1955, Volume 1, pg 17

11. Rokeach, M., *The Open and Closed Mind.* New York: Basic Books, 1960, pg 61

12. Hulbert, M., "The January Indicator: case against it still stands". *AAII Journal*, 1987, 9, no. 1

13. Hulbert, M., "The January Indicator: Fact or Fiction". *AAII Journal*, 1986, 8, no. 4

14. Dreman, D., *The New Contrarian Investment Strategy.* New York: Random House, 1982, pg 23

15. Wild, W.F., "Behavior modification: a therapeutic milieu for chronic schizophrenics". *Hawaii Medical Journal*, 1969, 29, no. 1

Chapter 2

1. Bales, R.F. "Task roles and social roles in problem-solving groups". In E.E. Maccoby, T.M. Newcomb, & E.L. Hartley (Eds.), *Readings in Social Psychology.* (3rd ed.) New York: Holt, 1958

2. Brown, R., *Social Psychology.* New York: The Free Press, 1965, pg 688

3. Hahn, A., Undated circular. Hume Financial Education Services, Received March 1987

Chapter 3

1. Samuelson, P.A., *Economics.* (4th ed.) New York: McGraw-Hill, 1958, pgs 275-276

2. Veblen, T., *The Theory of the Leisure Class.* New York: Mentor Books, 1957

Chapter 4

1. Paton, W.A., and Paton, Jr. W.A., *Corporation Accounts and Statements.* New York: MacMillan, 1955

2. Hunt, P., Williams, C.M., and Donaldson, G., *Basic Business Finance.* Illinois: Richard Irwin, Inc., 1958

3. Jordan, D.F., and Dougall, H.E., *Investments* (6th ed.). Englewood Cliffs, New Jersey: Prentice-Hall 1952

4. Guthmann, H.G. and Dougall, H.E., *Corporate Financial Policy* (3rd ed.), Englewood Cliffs, New Jersey: Prentice-Hall 1958

5. Sauvain, H., *Investment Management.* (2nd ed.), Englewood Cliffs, New Jersey: Prentice-Hall, 1959

6. Saint-Peter, N., "Options: The concept of equivalent strategies". AA# Journal, 1985, 7, no 7, pgs 15-18

7. 'Investor workshop—Part 1: Using stock market index futures, options on index futures, and options on a market index to manage your stock portfolio." *AAII Journal*, 1983, 5, no. 5, pgs 28-31

Chapter 5

1. Dowrie, G.W. and Fuller, D.R. *Investments* (2nd ed.), New York: Wiley & Sons, 1949, pg 10

2. Graham, B., *The Intelligent Investor* (4th ed.), New York: Harper and Row, 1973, pg 139

3. Cantwell, E.K., Chambers D.R., and Zdanowicz, "Brokers vs. Customers: What are your legal rights?" *AAII Journal*, 1987, 9, no. 3, pg 10

4. Zweig, M.E., *A Guide to Market Forecasting*. New York: Zweig Securities Advisory Service, 1987, pg 10

5. Dreman, D., *The New Contrarian Investment Strategy*. New York: Random House, 1982, pg 33-34

6. Malkiel, B.G., *A Random Walk Down Wall Street*. New York: Norton, 1973

7. Zweig, M. E., *Investor Expectations: Why they are the key to stock market trends.* New York. Zweig Securities Advisory Service, 1976

8. Bernhard, A., *Evaluating Common Stocks*. New York: Arnold Bernhard, 1979

9. Graham, B., *The Intelligent Investor* (4th ed.), New York: Harper and Row, 1973, pgs 119-120

10. American Association of Individual Investors, *The Individual Investor's Guide to No-Load Mutual Funds*. (6th ed.) Chicago: International Publishing Corp., 1987, pgs 35-37

11. Ibid, pg ix

Chapter 6

1. Dowrie, G. W. and Fuller, D. R. *Investments* (2nd ed.), New York: Wiley & Sons, 1949, pg 10

2. Homer, *The Odyssey*. Book XII. In Elliot, C.W., (Ed.), The Harvard Classics. New York: P.F. Collier & Son, 1909

3. Samuelson, P.A., *Economics*. (4th ed.) New York: McGraw-Hill, 1958, pgs 285-286

4. Ibid, pgs 579-585

5. *Value Line Investment Survey*, April 13, 1984, Supplement: "A Long Term Perspective". New York: Value Line Publishing, Inc.

6. Ibid, July 25, 1986, Selection & Opinion, "Market Monitor" New York: Value Line Publishing, Inc.

7. Samuelson, P.A., *Economics*. (4th ed.) New York. McGraw-Hill, 1958, pg 268

8. Smith, E.L., *Common stocks as Long Term Investment*. New York: MacMillan, 1926, pg 87

Chapter 7

1. Holloway, C. and Robert, J.C., "The role of the investment newsletter". *AAII Journal*, 1986, 8, no. 9, pg 18

2. Sauvain, H., *Investment Management.* (2nd ed.), Englewood Cliffs, New Jersey: Prentice-Hall, 1959, pg 7

3. Ibid, pg 109

4. Dreman, D., *The New Contrarian Investment Strategy.* New York: Random House, 1982, pgs 39-59

5. Scott, M.C., "How financial analysts interpret information". *AAII Journal,* 1986, 8, no. 5, pgs 10-12

6. Dohmen-Ramirez, B., "Liquidity the key to market activity". *The Honolulu Star Bulletin.* June 26, 1987

7. Graham, B., *The Intelligent Investor* (4th ed.), New York: Harper and Row, 1973, pg 14

8. Smith, E. L., *Common stocks as Long Term Investments.* New York: McMillan, 1926

9. *Value Line Investment Survey,* 1998, Supplement: "A Long Term Perspective". New York: Value Line Publishing, Inc.

Chapter 8

1. Dreman, D., *The New Contrarian Investment Strategy.* New York: Random House, 1982, pgs 19-37

2. Ibid, pgs 63-94

3. Sharp, R.M., "Equity valuation: An inflation, earnings and Beta model". AAII Journal, 1983, 5, no. 3, pg 14

4. Ibid, pgs 13-18

5. Festinger, L., *A Theory of Cognitive Dissonance.* Stanford, California: Stanford University Press, 1957, pg 33

Chapter 9

1. *Value Line Investment Survey,* 1998, Supplement: 'A Long Term Perspective.' New York: Value Line Publishing, Inc.

2. *Value Line Investment Survey*, June 5, 1987, Selection & Opinion, 'Quarterly Economic Review.' New York-Value Line Publishing, Inc.

3. Dowrie, G.W. and Fuller, D.R., *Investments* (2nd ed.), New York: Wfley & Sons, 1949, pgs 151-152

4. Samuelson, P.A., *Economics*. (4th ed.) New York: McGraw-Hill, 1958, pg 268

5. Smith, E.L., *Common stocks as Long Term Investments*, 1926, pgs 87-88

6. Bernahard, A., *Value Line Methods of Evaluating Common Stocks*. New York: Arnold Bernhard & Co., Inc., 1979

Chapter 10

1. *Value Line Investment Survey*, 1995, Supplement: 'A Long Term Perspective.' New York: Value Line Publishing, Inc.

2. *Value Line Investment Survey*, 1984, Supplement: 'A Long Term Perspective.' New York: Value Line Publishing, Inc.

3. *Value Line Investment Survey*, July 25, 1986, Selection & Opinion, 'Market Monitor." New York: Value Line Publishing, Inc.

4. Bernhard, A., *Value Line Methods of Evaluating Common Stock*, New York-Arnold Bernhard & Co., Inc., 1979

5. Scott, M.C., "Putting transaction costs into perspective". *AAII Journal*, 1987, 9, no. 1, pg 17

6. Hulbert, M., "Holding vs. Trading: The difference that time makes". AAII Journal, 1985, 7, no. 1

7. Epictetus, *The Enchiridion*. New York: Liberal Arts Press, 1948

8. Marcus Aurelius, *The Meditations of Marcus Aurelius*. In Elliot, C.W., (Ed.) The Harvard Classics. New York:. P.F. Collier & Son, 1909

9. Kelly, G., *The Psychology of Personal Constructs*. New York: W.W. Norton, 1955

10. Ellis, A., *Reason and emotion in psychotherapy*. New York: Lyle Stuart, 1962

11. Beck, A.T., *Cognitive therapy and the emotional disorders*. New York: International Universities Press, 1976

12. Beck, A.T., Rush, A.J., Shaw, B. F., and Emery, G., *Cognitive therapy of depression*. New York: Guilford Press, 1979, pgs 354-396

13. Frankl, V., *Man's search for meaning*. New York: Washington Square Press, 1963

14. Burns, D.D., *Feeling good. The new mood therapy*. New York: New American Library, 1980

Chapter 12

1. Trow, W.C., "The psychology of confidence". Archives of Psychology, 1923, 67, pgs 3-47

2. Johnson, D.M., "Confidence and achievement in eight branches of knowledge". *Journal of Educational Psychology*, 1941, 32, pgs 23-36

3. Block, J., and Petersen, P., "Some personality correlates of confidence, caution, and speed in a decision situation". *Journal of Abnormal and Social Psychology*, 1955, 51, pgs 34-41

4. Graham, B., *The Intelligent Investor* (4th ed.), New York: Harper and Row, 1973, pg 287

Chapter 13

1. *Value Line Investment Survey*, August 14, 1987, Selection & Opinion, "The Value Line Industrial Composite". New York: Value Line Publishing, Inc. pg 468

Glossary of Terms

ARBITRAGE—Arbitrage refers to the activity of making a profit from discrepancies between related markets by simultaneous purchase in one and sale in the other. Arbitrageurs thus provide an inadvertent service in keeping related markets in equilibrium.

BEAR—An investor who believes a sustained fall in market prices is imminent or in process.

BEAR MARKET—A market with falling prices continuing indefinitely.

BLUE CHIP—The stock of a large, well-established, and prospering corporation having good financial strength.

BONDS—A bond represents evidence of debt. Corporate bondholders are thus creditors of the company. A bond is an obligation to repay the principal sum at a stipulated time, which is called the date of maturity. It usually is also an obligation to pay periodic interest, normally semiannually.

BULL—An investor who believes a sustained rise in market prices is imminent or in process.

BULL MARKET—A market with rising prices continuing indefinitely.

CALL—An option to buy a stock at a specified price before a certain date.

CALL PROVISION—Some bonds and preferred stock confer the right to the issuer to "call" (discharge) the issue after a specified time for redemption at a specified price.

CDs—Nickname for certificates of deposit.

CERTIFICATES OF DEPOSIT—Certificates of deposit are issued by a bank or savings institution and may generally be considered either as nonmarketable original issue discount bonds or as <u>time-limited</u> savings accounts. Often called CDs, they normally pay a higher rate of interest than savings accounts to compensate for the decreased liquidity.

CHURNING—The improper practice of promoting excessive trading to generate commissions for the inappropriate enrichment of a broker.

COMMON STOCK—Common stock is the pristine and most complete form of corporate ownership. Its primary characteristics are the following: (1) a residual claim on assets and income, (2) participation in growth, and (3) voting power. Although infrequent, sometimes special classes of common stock are created by a company's charter, which alters the stock's characteristics.

CONVERTIBLE SECURITIES—Convertible bonds and convertible preferred stock are hybrids. They may be changed in common stock at a specified ratio at the demand of the holder, thus having a potential claim on ownership and growth. Because of this, their performance as investments has dual features. They perform in some respects as common stock and in others as their original type, bond or preferred stock. This aspect of their performance is governed by the proximity to the conversion price and by the direction of the movement of the stock's price.

CORPORATE STOCK—Corporate stock represents ownership of the corporation. As owners, stockholders have a residual claim on their company's assets and income. Corporate stock may be common or preferred.

CORRELATION—A correlation tells us if and to what extent two things are related. The coefficient of correlation is a number that says how much the variations in one thing conform to the variations in another. The number can range from 0, which means no relationship, to 1, which means a perfect relationship or identity. The coefficient has a sign to indicate the direction of the relationship: a + means they move together while a—means they move in opposite directions. Correlations are subjected to a test to determine the likelihood that they are merely a chance finding. A statement that a correlation is <u>significant</u> means that the chances that the correlation arose by chance are so remote as to be comfortably rejected. The customary guidelines for remoteness are less than 1 in 100 (.01) or less than 5 in 500 (.05).

CURRENT ASSETS—Assets are things of value that are owned. Current assets are those that can or are expected to be converted into cash within the current period, usually one year or less.

CURRENT LIABILITIES—Liabilities are things that are owed. Current liabilities are those that are required to be paid within the current period, usually one year.

CURRENT RATIO—Current assets divided by current liabilities. This ratio is used to describe the liquidity (sufficiency of cash to meet current needs) of a company. *Current* refers to the present short-term period, usually a year.

DEBENTURE—Debentures are bonds that are not secured by a lien on specific assets. Holders rely upon the general credit of the issuer.

DILUTION—The decrease in proportional ownership of each share of stock due to an increase in the number of shares. This may occur from the exercise of stock options, the conversion of convertible issues, or the issuance of additional stock. Dilution is accompanied by an immediate decrease in the value represented by the stock.

ELASTIC—The tendency of sales to respond sharply to changes in price.

EQUITIES—Ownership rights in property—for example, common stock in corporations, ownership units in partnerships, and excess of real property value above any mortgage obligation.

FEDERAL DEPOSIT INSURANCE CORPORATION—Also known as the FDIC, this is a federal agency charged with providing insurance for bank accounts.

FEDERAL SAVINGS AND LOAN INSURANCE CORPORATION—A federal agency, also known as the FSLIC, charged with providing insurance for savings and loan association savings accounts.

FIRST MORTGAGE BOND—Bonds secured by a primary lien on specific assets of the issuer.

FUTURES CONTRACTS—A binding legal agreement to buy or sell something at a certain date in the future at a specified price. That something may be a commodity to be delivered later or a financial abstraction that is incapable of delivery.

INELASTIC—The tendency of sales to have a muted response to changes in price.

INTEREST—The monetary reimbursement for the temporary use of money.

INVESTMENT BANKER—A banker who initiates the sale of security issues. His customer is the organization, usually corporation or governmental unit, desiring to issue the security.

LEVERAGE—A device by which one increases the potential for gains or losses from an investment. Usually this is done by adding borrowed funds to one's own when investing. The same end may be achieved by trading in issues like warrants that have a price with a small base but a large potential for change.

LIMIT ORDER—An order to buy or sell securities may be either on a market or limit basis. On limit orders, the investor specifies a price that may not be violated. When selling, the sale must not be for less; when buying, no more may be paid. The contrasting market order specifies only that the order be executed immediately at the best currently available price.

LIQUIDITY—The sufficiency of the ability to generate cash to satisfy current obligations for payments. It is frequently measured by the current ratio. It consists of cash, cash equivalents, and things that may readily be converted to cash.

LOAD—The commission charged by some mutual funds for placing money into the fund, also a fee charged to withdraw from the fund.

MARGIN—A type of purchase made through a broker on other than cash terms. The buyer deposits a portion of the price of the security and the broker lends the remainder. The broker requires a certain portion of the value of the securities kept on deposit; hence, if the security declines in price, an additional cash deposit will be required. If the additional cash is not forthcoming, the securities will be sold and the account closed.

MARKET ORDER—An order to buy or sell securities may be either on a market or limit basis. "At the market" requests an immediate order at the best currently available price, while a limit order specifies a price that must not be violated downward in a sale or upward in a purchase.

MUNICIPAL BONDS—Bonds issued by all nonfederal governments within the United States. This includes those obligations of the various states, counties, townships, taxation districts, and agencies of state and local governments. Municipal bonds deemed "public issues" are nontaxable by the federal government.

NEGOTIABLE SECURITIES—Pledges or acknowledgments of property rights that may be freely bought or sold.

NONSYSTEMATIC RISK—Risk that comes from specific sources that do not influence an entire market. They may be specific in their impact only to one company, industry, or region.

ODD LOT—An odd lot is a transaction involving fewer than one hundred shares.

OPTION—A contract conferring the right to buy or sell securities at specified prices within a stated time.

OTC—Abbreviation for *over-the-counter*.

OVER-THE-COUNTER—A term used to described the market for securities that were not sold on organized security exchanges. It has now become organized under the name NASDAQ and is composed of thousands of dealers around the country operating out of their own offices who are in touch with other dealers in a communications network.

p—A statistical abbreviation for probability. Thus the expression $p < .01$ is read as follows: the probability is less than 1 in 100.

P/E—Abbreviation of price/earnings ratio.

PREFERRED STOCK—A class of stock having a priority in claim on assets and income over the claims of common stockholders. In the payment of dividends, and in the distribution of assets upon liquidation, the preferred stockholders' claims must be completely satisfied before anything goes to common stockholders. Their position is a curious hybrid between creditors and owners, or between owners of bonds and common stock. They are properly considered stock because their claims may simply be put aside if insufficient funds exist. Yet they may be thought of as creditors, because they receive a stipulated yield and do not share in growth or decision making.

PRICE/EARNINGS RATIO—The price of a stock divided by its earnings per share. This ratio is a basic measure of how cheap or expensive a stock is.

PUT—An option to sell stock at a specified price before a certain date.

r—A statistical symbol for the Pearson coefficient of correlation. The statement that $r = +.87$ means that the correlation, as computed by the Pearson method, is a positive one whose value is .87. The value of r can vary from 1 (a perfect relationship) to 0 (the absence of a relationship). In a positive relationship, the elements move together like smoking and cancer; in a negative relationship, they move in opposite directions like smoking and longevity.

r^2—The square of r, i.e., r multiplied by itself, r^2, is also called the variance and reflects the proportion of variation of one of the variables that is associated with a variation in the other.

$r_{12.3}$—The symbol for the coefficient of partial correlation, in which one removes from the relationship of variables #1 and #2, any influence attributable to variable #3.

RIGHTS—Rights to purchase a portion of a new issue of common stock at prices below the market price may be issued by a corporation to its existing stockholders. Such rights therefore have a distinct market value and may be either exercised or traded in their own right until their expiration date, after which they no longer have value. They are utilized to simultaneously facilitate the issuance of additional stock and protect the rights of their stockholders to the preservation of proportional interest in the corporation.

SECURITY—(1) A written obligation, evidence, or document of ownership or creditorship—as a stock, bond, note, debenture, certificate, etc.—acknowledging the holder's right to the specified property. Securities may or may not be negotiable; (2) collateral pledged to the repayment of a bond or other debt.

SHORT INTEREST—The number of shares that have been sold short and not yet repurchased.

SHORT SALE—A sale of stock that one does not own but has borrowed from a broker. As a loan, it must be repaid. This is done by subsequently buying the stock or covering one's short position.

STOCK MARKET INDEX FUTURES—These are a specific form of futures contract. They are a recent innovation and function similarly to commodities futures, except of course that there is nothing to deliver apart from a payment, the amount of which is determined by the interim performance of the particular stock index used.

σ—Symbol for standard deviation, which is the major statistical indicator of variability or dispersion of a group of data. It is the square root of the average of the squared deviations of each datum from the mean.

SYSTEMATIC RISK—Risk that comes from influences that simultaneously affect essentially an entire market. Such influences may be thought of as tides lifting or casting down everything in the market. The following types of risks have wholly or partially systematic effects: interest rate risk, economic risk, and risks attaching to psychological climate.

TREASURY BILL—Federal debt instrument with the shortest term. Treasury bills mature typically in ninety or ninety-one days from date of issues. They are issued at a discount from face value. The interest is received when the bill is sold and is the difference between the amount paid and the amount received at sale.

TREASURY BOND—(1) A generic term meaning any federal debt security; (2) long-term federal debt issued with maturities that vary from five to forty years and with interest paid periodically. These bonds often have call provisions.

TREASURY NOTE—An intermediate-term federal debt instrument, maturing in from one to five years. Interest is paid periodically.

WARRANTS—Stock purchase warrants entitle the holder to buy common stock from the issuer at a certain price. Their exercise may be limited in time or may run indefinitely. Warrants may or may not be listed for trading on a stock exchange in their own right.

YIELD—A measure of the size of a periodic payment of an investment in relation to the size of the investment. It is calculated by adding the payments (dividends or interest) received in a year and dividing by the price. It is usually expressed as a percentage.

YIELD TO MATURITY—A measure of the full yield on a bond with a life longer than one year. To the calculation of current yield (interest divided by cost of the bond), a portion is added or subtracted to represent the yearly amortization of the discount under or premium over the par value that will eventually be received at maturity.

Index

7740998R0

Made in the USA
Lexington, KY
13 December 2010